All About
Heroin

All About
Heroin

BEN SONDER

FRANKLIN WATTS
A Division of Scholastic Inc.
New York • Toronto • London • Auckland • Sydney
Mexico City • New Delhi • Hong Kong
Danbury, Connecticut

Interior Design by Molly Heron
Photographs © 2002: AP/Wide World Photos: 13 (Ricardo Mazalan), 113
(Kathy Willens); Archive Photos/Getty Images: 55 (Arcieri/Reuters), 59
(Lee Celano/Reuters), 88 (CNP), 10 (Vincent West/Reuters), 62, 70;
Custom Medical Stock Photo/John Smith: 40; Photo Researchers, NY: 36
inset (Van Bucher), 25 (Oscar Burriel/SPL), 21 (Alain Dex/Publiphoto), 66
(David R. Frazier), 103 (M.E. Warren), 51 (Garry Watson/SPL); PhotoEdit: 49
(Myrleen Ferguson), 31 right (Anna E. Zuckerman); Photofest: 26, 74;
The Image Works/Charles Gatewood: 63; Visuals Unlimited: 31 left
(Bob Newman), 36 (Erwin C. "Bud" Nielsen).

Pie Chart and Graphs by Kathleen Hamilton

Library of Congress Cataloging-in-Publication Data

Sonder, Ben, 1954-
    All about heroin / Ben Sonder.
        p. cm.
    Includes bibliographical references and index.
    ISBN 0-531-11541-0
        1. Heroin habit—Juvenile literature. 2. Heroin—History—
Juvenile literature. 3. Heroin—Physiological effect—Juvenile literature.
[1. Heroin. 2. Drug Abuse.] I. Title.

HV5822.H4 S65 2002
363.29'3—dc21

Contents

All About
Heroin

Chapter 1

The Heroin Experience

Summer 1996. Fans of the post-Grunge alternative rock group Smashing Pumpkins had been waiting for months. Finally, the big moment was drawing near. In another 24 hours the group would be onstage in Manhattan's Madison Square Garden before an audience of thousands. Their two shows at the Garden had been sold out for weeks. Even though the group wasn't as big as Nirvana had been, it had thousands of hardcore followers.

As a matter of fact, there really seemed to be no such thing as a halfway Smashing Pumpkins fan. If you were into them, you were into them all the way. It was a heavy-duty trip, and you felt as if you knew them intimately. Lyrics like "I'm in love with my sadness" or "despite all my rage, I am still just a rat in a cage" struck a chord in devoted Smashing Pumpkins fans. The words made even more sense if you'd

Smashing Pumpkins

followed some of the band members from earlier incarnations, when they played what they called "gloomy art rock." Their music was all about angst, alienation, outrage and dark beauty. Their distorted guitar chords, romantic string arrangements and black-mood lyrics said everything about being an outsider.

Some fans, but not all of them, knew how closely the band's life style mirrored their songs. The drummer, Jimmy Chamberlain, had been to rehab for alcohol and heroin. And the singer for the Smashing Pumpkins, Billy Corgan, had had a nervous collapse in 1992. But nobody predicted how bad things could get on the night before the first concert at the Garden. At about 11 P.M. on a Thursday, July 11,[1] the band's keyboard player, Jonathan Melvoin, arrived at the Regency Hotel on 61st Street with Jimmy Chamberlain. The two began injecting heroin and at some point both fell into a deep nod—a mental state similar to sleep. Jimmy woke up in the middle of the night and noticed that Jonathan had passed out completely. After nothing he did could wake him, including dragging him into a cold shower, Jimmy called the police. Jonathan had overdosed. He was dead.

Fans got the news about a day and a half later. There wouldn't be any concerts at Madison Square Garden tomorrow or the next day. A lot of people were in shock.

Well, kind of in shock. In some ways it was par for the course. The rock music profession had always been tainted with heroin problems. Jimi Hendrix and Janis Joplin, the Red Hot Chili Peppers, Kurt Cobain—all of them had struggled with the drug, and some of them had died from it. Still, there were idealistic fans of the Smashing Pumpkins who couldn't believe what had happened. What, they wondered, had gone on in the heads of Melvoin and Chamberlain the night they stuck needles into their arms? How could they have taken such a chance? How much could they have cared about their talent to put their lives in danger?

Hopefully, this book will help you understand the choices they and other people make when they use heroin. You'll find out what heroin feels like and why people keep using it. And you'll also discover what it does to the body on both a short-term and long-term basis. You'll get up-to-the-minute

---

[1] Neil Strauss, "Musician for Smashing Pumpkins Dies of Apparent Drug Overdose," *New York Times*, July 13, 1996, Metropolitan Desk, archives.

information on heroin trends and the life styles of heroin users, as well as the history of heroin. You'll learn how the government and police are trying to deal with it. And finally, you'll learn about the treatment options.

WHAT IS HEROIN?

Heroin is a chemical processed from a natural substance that can be extracted from many varieties of poppy plants. That natural substance is opium, a latex-like fluid that is excreted by the poppy seed pod. The species of poppy traditionally used for opium is the *Papaver somniferum*, an annual plant, but most species of poppies contain some opium. The majority of strong pain-killers that exist today are produced from parts of the opium poppy. They are used by hospitals and pharmacies to treat moderate to severe pain. Their use in medicine has proved invaluable in the last several hundred years, and no more effective substance for killing pain has ever been discovered. The natural alkaloids of the opium poppy are the well-known narcotics, morphine and codeine. But the opium poppy is also used in the production of semi-synthetic narcotics, such as heroin, hydromorphone, and oxycodone.

It should be understood that the opium poppy is not the only source of narcotics. However, the chemical structure of opium is at the basis for several other opiate-like drugs that chemically resemble the substances extracted from opium but that are produced totally synthetically. Taken together, these drugs, which are either derived from opium or similar to the alkaloids found within it, are all called *opioids*.

Only the pod, or seed-holding part of the poppy plant, can produce opium. This substance comes from within the walls of the ovary of the plant and oozes out if a "ripe" pod

Anti-narcotic police officers in Colombia examine the bulb of a poppy flower.

is sliced with a sharp knife. Illegal growers of the opium poppy in the hills of Southeast Asia all use a method to extract opium from the seed pod that was developed hundreds of years ago. They slit the plant seed pods with a knife and carefully collect the latex-like ooze from it. As this whitish substance slowly dries, the water passes out of it and forms a brown, sticky gum. The gum is almost pure opium, which can be smoked, eaten, or transformed into other substances.

SOME OPIOID DRUGS*

OPIOID	CHARACTERISTICS	USE
OPIOIDS OF NATURAL ORIGIN		
Opium	Dark-brown gum that is produced by drying the fluid from the opium seed pod	Contains alkaloids needed to produce morphine, codeine, heroin, and other opioids; used in past for diarrhea and as a tranquilizer; smoked illegally for the high
Morphine	White crystal; odorless, bitter taste; principal constituent of opium (4 to 21%)	One of the most effective drugs known for the relief of pain; injected; also abused by addicts
Codeine	Alkaloid found in raw opium (0.7 to 2.5%); provides less analgesia than morphine	Relieves moderate pain and cough; occasionally abused for the high
SEMI-SYNTHETIC OPIOIDS		
Heroin	Synthesized from morphine; white to dark brown depending on additives and method of preparation	Illegal in the U.S.; used for the high

---

* Some of the information in this chart was adapted from Narcotic Identification Manual, U.S. Government Printing Office, 1988—544-809

OPIOID	CHARACTERISTICS	USE
Hydromorphone (Dilaudid)**	Tablet or injectable form; shorter-acting than morphine but 2 to 8 times as potent	Prescribed for severe pain; abused by addicts
Oxycodone (Percodan, Percocet)	Synthesized from thebaine, a minor constituent of opium; similar to codeine but more potent and more addictive	Prescribed for moderate to severe pain; dissolved, filtered out, and injected by addicts
Etorphine	Synthesized from thebaine; more than 1,000 times more potent than morphine	Used to immobilize large wild animals
WHOLLY SYNTHETIC OPIOIDS		
Meperidine (Demerol)	First synthetic narcotic; administered either orally or by injection	Most widely prescribed drug for severe pain; abused by addicts

---

** Trade names are enclosed by parentheses. Sometimes a trade name denotes a drug with more than one ingredient. For example, "Percodan" contains oxycodone, terephthalate, and aspirin.

OPIOID	CHARACTERISTICS	USE
Methadone	Synthesized in Germany during World War II; effects last longer than morphine-based drugs (up to 24 hours)	Administered orally to control narcotic addiction; abused by addicts, who buy and sell it as a street drug
Levo-alpha-acetylmethadol (LAMM)	Like methadone, but duration is 48 to 72 hours	Used to control narcotic addiction; long duration means fewer visits to clinic
Propoxyphene (Darvon)	Chemically similar to methadone; less effective as a pain-killer than other opioids but also less addictive	Prescribed for relief of mild to moderate pain
Fentanyl	The most potent narcotic that is used clinically in the U.S. (50 to 100 times more potent than morphine)	Injected for anesthesia and severe pain; patch used for chronic severe pain; additive in street heroin that can cause users to overdose
Tramadol (Ultram)	One of the newest synthetic opioids; tablets; more effective at relieving pain than codeine but less effective at relieving pain than codeine + aspirin; some potential for addiction	For moderate to moderately severe pain

Growers in the centers of legal opium cultivation in India, Turkey, Tasmania, and Australia tend to use a more modern method. They process the entire plant and extract at least 125 different alkaloids from it. From these alkaloids are made opiates and other opiate-related synthetic drugs.

Heroin can't be made directly from raw opium. It's not a naturally occurring alkaloid but a semi-synthetic derivative. To make heroin, first morphine must be extracted from the opium. This extraction is often accomplished using hot water, lime, and ammonium chloride. Once pure morphine has been obtained, it can be converted to heroin by heating it with acetic anhydride, which is a common industrial acid, after which impurities are filtered out. The process produces a chemically bonded synthesis between the acetic anhydride and the morphine. This substance is a white crystal whose chemical structure is $C_{21}H_{23}NO_5$ and whose chemical name is diacetylmorphine, or heroin. Depending on details in the preparation process, the heroin produced can be injected, sniffed, or smoked. It may reach the user in its white crystal state, or it may arrive in a state closer to raw opium—a brownish-black, tar-like gum. The white crystal, or white powder, form of heroin is usually sold on the street in a small plastic envelope or in a folded piece of white paper. The black tar form often comes in a deflated balloon, which can be torn or cut open to get the sticky tar inside. Heroin is more powerful than morphine. The acidic bond in heroin fortifies the morphine, making it at least ten times more powerful than morphine alone.

In almost no case, however, does heroin reach users in pure form. To get to users, the drug has to pass from the producer to a series of less and less powerful middlemen, all of whom cut the heroin they receive with cheaper substances in order to make more money. Some of the cutting

HEROIN's CHEMICAL CHARACTERISTICS

NAME	Diacetylmorphine
CHEMICAL NAME	(5alpha,6alpha)-7,8-Didehydro-4,5-epoxy-17-methylmorphinan-3,6-diol diacetate (ester)
ALTERNATE **CHEMICAL NAMES**	heroin, diamorphine, acetomorphine
CHEMICAL FORMULA	C21H23NO5
MOLECULAR WEIGHT	369.42
MELTING POINT	243-244° (hydrochloride monohydrate-fine crystals)

From the *Merck Index,* 12th Edition

substances for the white powder type include talcum powder, milk sugar, baby laxative, quinine, baking soda, strychnine, the very powerful synthetic opiate fentanyl, and dozens of other harmless and harmful substances. Nevertheless, the current trend is toward purer heroin, a factor that has led to increasing overdoses among users.

WHAT IS TAKING HEROIN LIKE?

Some people who use heroin prefer the rush they get from injecting, or "mainlining," it directly into a vein. Others prefer to inject it under the skin or intramuscularly, which produces a more gradual high. Some always sniff ("snort") it, which is an even more gradual way of feeling its effects. Still others smoke it by putting a trail of the powder on a sheet of tin foil and heating it with a match held underneath the foil, inhaling the vaporized heroin with a pipette or barrel from a ballpoint pen. Smoking heroin in this way is popularly referred to as "chasing the dragon." In all cases, the effects come quite rapidly. Mainlining heroin is the fastest route. It delivers the chemical to the brain in about 8 seconds. Smoking heroin is another rapid way to ingest it; intramuscular injection takes about 6 minutes to work its effects. Sniffed heroin peaks in about 10 or 15 minutes.[2]

Once heroin reaches the brain, its effects take over the entire body. Subjective reports vary. There are those who say it produces the greatest rush of pleasure they've ever experienced. Others who have tried the drug are not that impressed by the effects. They describe it as a dulling, a forced "slowing down" that takes control of one's motor skills and reflexes. Still others have found it to be a nightmare drug because of its side effects, which can include intense vomiting shortly after it reaches the brain, allergic itching as the drug takes hold, and a sense of severe, sometimes frightening disorientation. However, the devoted heroin lover insists on the more sensational descriptions of the drug, often describing the "rush" as an irresistible wave of warmth spreading through the fibers of every muscle. This may be accompanied by a sense of well-being and profound relaxation, or, in some users, by a pleasant feeling of energy. That energy may be related to heroin's reputation as a euphoric, a drug that can temporarily create a sensation of heightened joy. But heroin does not always create such an effect for all people or for the same person all the time. In

---

[2] "Heroin," NIDA Research Report Series, National Institutes of Health, U.S. Department of Health and Human Services.

fact, the psychological effects of the opiate experience are unpredictable and seem to depend a great deal on the setting. We are used to hearing about the "euphoria" of opiates, but doctors and nurses know that strong opiates, such as morphine, can create restlessness, paranoia, hallucinations, and anguish in some patients.

In most but not all cases, a strong dose of heroin, taken in a setting chosen by the user, will discourage activity. Although heroin seriously disrupts motor skills and creates slurred speech only when taken in amounts close to overdose, the user of even a small amount is often content with just slumping in a chair or lying down to concentrate on the effects. Those who have taken dangerously strong doses will often sway forward and backward on their feet as if about to topple. People on heroin may become talkative or introspective, but either state may take on a special blurred perfection, as if it never felt so full or so whole.

This doesn't mean that the user who is high becomes immune to annoyances. Events that jolt heroin users temporarily out of their highs can be extremely unsettling for some users. Sometimes they produce aggressive reactions. This is often the case for twenty-year-old James,[3] a New Yorker who is a long-term heroin user. He was introduced to mainlining the drug at twelve by his now-deceased father, who himself had been a user for twenty years. James says that heroin has its spectacular and euphoric peaks for him, except when someone interferes. For example, if someone taps him on the shoulder while he is nodding out in a park or swaying on his feet on a bus, he will suddenly become

---

[3] The anecdotes and subjective reports about heroin users in this book are based on interviews or anecdotal information collected by the author. Names have been changed.

irrationally hostile and maybe even take a swing at the person. James has also had to endure another upsetting side effect of the drug. As it wears off, he sometimes goes into seizures similar to those experienced by an epileptic.

Those who choose to be inactive after injecting heroin inevitably fall into a nod. The eyelids become heavy and begin to close; when they close all the way, the head may drop to the chest. The user leaves the conscious world for seconds or minutes at a time, during which deep dreamlike reveries, or merely a state that is like sleep, occur. Sometimes the dreamlike reveries are extremely pleasant and interesting. At other times, the nods feel as if they are being forced on the user against his will, a frightening sensation akin to the feeling of fainting. This may cause the user to jerk out of the nod as if startled. An abrupt realization of where he is, or an unexpected sound or touch, can produce the same sudden, startled effect in the user.

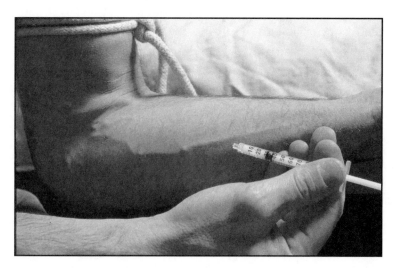

This addict has tied off his upper arm in order to find a vein with which to mainline heroin.

Since heroin is a strong pain-killer, petty, chronic physical annoyances that may have bothered the user before a dose, such as backaches, a foot blister, or arthritic joints, seem miraculously to have disappeared. If the user has a chronic cough, the heroin suppresses the brain activity that sets it off, so it may seem as if the cough has disappeared.

Because heroin dulls a multitude of sensations and stimulates pleasure-producing chemicals in the brain, it can have an effect on the emotions and even on the moral sense. Heroin users are able to feel that everything is roses in the worst situations. Joey, an eighteen-year-old who has been a heroin smoker for two years, says that heroin makes him "ready to do anything." He works in Manhattan as a male prostitute, which he says he endures by "staying high." He also stated, "When I'm high I could do anything to get more. Anything, man. Rob somebody. Hurt them. It don't matter none to me cause it's like you're doing it in a dream. Everything is so smooth!"

But heroin doesn't only numb one's reactions to others' pain. It can also curtail self-awareness, inhibit one's sense of timing, or eliminate feelings of propriety. Nancy, who is thirty-eight years old, has been shooting heroin on New York's Lower East Side for almost twenty years. Most of her time awake is spent high. Until a few years ago, she would customarily go to her friend Marsha's apartment to shoot up with her. Then, about two years ago, Marsha, who has full-blown AIDS, was moved from her apartment to a hospice. Like a Pavlovian trained lab animal, Nancy cannot break the old association between being at Marsha's and getting high. Now, each day, two years after Marsha has been gone, Nancy still comes to the building to get high. The only trouble is, the building is now a renovated co-op. So Nancy squats in the entranceway, partially hidden from the sidewalk, using a match to melt her heroin mixed with a little water in a bottle cap. When the heroin has dissolved, she must look for a good vein. Since those in her arms have long ago collapsed from too many punctures, she generally searches for one in her upper thigh, which means she must lower her slacks. More often than not, her shot is strong enough to send her into an instantaneous nod. Sometimes, before she has come to, one of the current residents of the co-op finds her in the entranceway, her pants down and her shooting gear next to her. She is shooed away, usually before she has time to pull herself together. But the next day, the same thing happens all over again. Nancy is too numb to worry about the embarrassment. And being high makes her lose track of time. She plans to leave quickly. She isn't aware that she's nodding out and hasn't left yet. And finally, her brain is too anesthetized for her to think of another plan.

TOLERANCE TO HEROIN

How much heroin is needed to feel the effects that have just been described? There is no simple answer to that question. Factors include the physiology of the user's body and the setting. They depend on how long the user has been taking heroin. They also depend on how pure the dose is. These uncertainties are a major factor in the dangers of taking heroin. From day to day a user cannot be certain how he or she will react to the drug. Will it produce a high? Will it send the user into a coma? Regular heroin use is a scenario of constant experimentation.

An important factor in all that uncertainty is increasing tolerance to the drug. Tolerance is declining reactivity to a drug in proportion to the number of times it is taken. Heroin produces tolerance. This means that the euphoric effect will require stronger and stronger doses. So will all the other aspects of the heroin experience. None of these effects can occur until the amount of heroin has reached a saturation that goes beyond the tolerance threshold. A strong tolerance to the drug means large amounts of it are needed. It is a sign of addiction to the drug and the promise that if it is stopped, withdrawal symptoms will occur.

COMING DOWN

The analgesic and dreamlike effects of heroin continue over a period of several hours. Then they slowly wear off. If the user is not addicted, the comedown from heroin is merely a rude return to the annoyances of this world. The cough or headache one may have had before will come back. The nodding and reveries fade away. Muscle aches return, and, in most cases, anything that seemed bad about life before seems a little worse now. In general, opiates move quite slowly through the body's systems (though some types more slowly than others). The day after a person takes heroin, he or she may experience a heroin hangover that includes headache, weakness, dizziness, and fragile nerves.

For a regular user of heroin, the comedown signals an emergency. If the user has developed tolerance to a high enough degree, withdrawal sets in when the drug is discontinued. Addicts say that withdrawal begins as a dull, dead, cold feeling that makes one crave the lost warmth and placid feeling of the drug. If that craving is not satisfied, the more dramatic physical symptoms of withdrawal take over. Among regular users, symptoms of withdrawal can occur as soon as a few hours after the last dose. That is why seasoned heroin users have been known to inject as much as four or five times a day.

Headache and dizziness are two symptoms of a heroin hangover.

Again, subjective descriptions of real withdrawal vary widely. Filmmakers, novelists, journalists, and some addicts have portrayed it as a living hell. Some users, and recently, some medical researchers, have downplayed the severity of heroin withdrawal, pointing out that it is less dangerous than withdrawal from severe alcohol or barbiturate dependence. They claim that it mostly resembles the symptoms of a bad case of flu (muscle and bone aches and chills).

The first symptom of withdrawal is likely to be restlessness. The user can't stay still or find a comfortable position. He or she may jump up and start pacing, stab at an itch whose position keeps changing; or make jerky, convulsive movements. A person going into withdrawal may be

The 1971 film *The Panic in Needle Park*, starring Al Pacino, provides a stirring portrait of heroin abuse.

overcome by uncontrollable yawning, tearing, and perspiring as well as severe anxiety. Next may come muscle and bone pain, sometimes accompanied by twitching and cramping of the muscles and stomach cramps. At the same time, there may be a runny nose, diarrhea or vomiting, cold flashes with goose bumps, and involuntary kicking movements. The symptoms are at their worst 48 to 72 hours after quitting the drug. After a week, most of them have subsided.[4]

ACUTE INTOXICATION AND OVERDOSING

Acute intoxication with heroin means that the body has received the maximum of the dose it can tolerate. In the most extreme form of acute heroin intoxication, the user is likely to lose consciousness quickly. The nod becomes extended, and the person slips into a coma. Respiration slows to dangerous levels or stops altogether. Decreased respiration may make the fingers, toes, or lips turn blue. Attempts by fellow users or friends to revive the user (slapping, cold showers, trying to make the user walk, artificial respiration) may be successful if the intoxication is not too intense and if the user has not fallen into a deep coma. But in some cases, such as that of Jonathan Melvoin, the keyboard player for the Smashing Pumpkins, the user can't be revived.

There are warning signs of acute intoxication, but the user isn't always aware of them. Someone who is acutely intoxicated by heroin is likely to be in a state of euphoria or extreme restlessness. He or she will be flushed and have

---

[4] From "Heroin," Pamphlet 13548, National Institutes of Health (National Institute of Drug Abuse), U.S. Department of Health and Human Services.

clammy-feeling skin. Drowsiness, a decreased breathing rate, itching skin, and a slow pulse are all signs of advanced stages of the high. Whether these symptoms will lead to a more dangerous state of affairs or will simply diminish can't be predicted. Too many factors are involved, including the user's state of health and the environment where this is taking place.

HOW DO THE BODY SYSTEMS REACT TO HEROIN?

The subjective experiences are one thing, and observing them from the outside is another. But what is really going on in the body of a person who takes heroin? What causes the craving for it? What happens in the body during heroin withdrawal? For years researchers have studied the chemical and physical changes that take place during the administration of opiates. Only recently, however, have they begun to unveil the deepest workings of the opioids within the nervous system.

From a neurochemical and physiological point of view, this is the heroin experience: Shortly after the heroin crosses the blood-brain barrier, it is converted to 6-monoacetylmorphine and eventually to morphine. In the brain and nearby organs of the nervous system, the opiates go to work. They produce changes in the limbic system, which is responsible for emotional phenomena. Changes in the limbic system are probably the cause of the feeling of euphoria produced by heroin, but other changes in the same area of the brain are probably responsible for other emotional reactions, such as the violence that surges through James when someone disturbs his high.

When opiates spread through the nervous system, they

also begin to block pain messages sent by the spinal cord to the brain from the body. Then, by affecting the brain stem, which is the seat of many of the body's autonomic functions, opiates may also act to depress breathing and heart rate. Other functions affected include contractility in the digestive system, often leading to constipation; pupil dilation and constriction, which is why highly intoxicated heroin addicts have "pinpoint" pupils; and the muscular contractions of the bladder, which is why a user may find it difficult to urinate when he or she is high. All the other experiences of the heroin high—flushed skin, perspiration, dry mouth, decrease in blood pressure—are a result of essential changes in body functioning caused by messages from the nervous system. Heroin affects almost every single body system. Of course, if these effects are too acute, it means that the systems are virtually shutting down. The body may go into seizures or respiratory arrest and/or end up in a coma. Such a condition can lead to death by overdose.

THE OPIOID PEPTIDES

The first significant breakthrough in understanding heroin's effect on the brain occurred in the 1950s, when two researchers, J.W. Hughes and H.W. Kosterlitz, discovered two powerful pain-killing peptides in a pig's brain.[5] They called these substances enkephalins. Later, larger peptides that were related to the enkephalins—the so-called endorphins—were discovered. Both endorphins and enkephalins belong to a family of natural secretions within the body that

---

[5] "Drugs and Drug Action," Britannica CD, Version 99 © 1994–1999. Encyclopædia Britannica, Inc.

include, among other substances, the opioid peptides. That's right: our own body produces chemicals that are similar to opioids in structure. And when these chemicals bind with certain receptors in the brain, we experience pleasure.

The entire mechanism of pleasure-producing chemicals and the receptors for them probably evolved within us as survival devices. Imagine, for example, a hunting-gathering party composed of primitive prehumans. Perhaps a flash of color or a sound caught the senses of the hunter-gatherers and stimulated them to investigate. And suppose the investigation revealed fruit hanging from a tree. If the fruit tasted good, the experience released opioid peptides in the brain, signaling pleasure. If the fruit was bitter or in some other way unfit to eat, opioid peptides were not released. In this way, the peptides serve as guides to survival, motivating the hunter-gatherer to search for and eat a particular fruit since it is connected with a rush of pleasure.

But endorphins also perform another function. When the body experiences pain—a bruise, a wound, a toothache—the brain sends messages to release more endorphins. These pleasure-producing chemicals serve to counteract some of the pain sensation. It's as if we carried our own pain-killers within our bodies.

Opioid substances that are not produced by the body— morphine, heroin, and the other opioid pain-killers—may act similarly to opioid peptides once they are inside the body. They bind to the same receptors and produce a mood-altering sensation of pleasure. No stimulus, such as succulent fruit, is needed for this reaction. The opiates take over the role of pleasure-causing external stimuli.

The evolutionary description of hunting and gathering above may have a bearing on why opiates are addictive. We are programmed by evolution to return to those things that

Good, ripe fruit releases pleasure-producing chemicals in the brain; unripe, inedible fruit does not.

set off our pleasure chemicals. However, there is likely to be another, more sinister cause of opiate addiction. When an addict's nerve cells are repeatedly bombarded with high levels of pleasure-stimulating chemicals, they may rebel. To protect its tissues, the brain may reduce the number of receptors to which these chemicals can bind. This means that the brain, which now lacks a normal amount of pleasure receptors, will require more and more stimulation for the user to experience pleasure. When the bombardment of heroin's opioids ceases, the addict's ability to experience pleasure may drop to an intolerably low level. Depression, restlessness, and other negative feelings set in, and only more heroin can make the addict feel normal.[6]

Taking heroin is an immensely complicated physiological experience. It seems likely that the body has a whole battery of receptors for opioids, not just those receptors that produce the sensation of pleasure. It is currently believed that there are eight types of opiate receptors. The three most studied are the *mu* receptors, which control feelings of euphoria, depress respiration, block pain, and produce the reactions of physical addiction; the *kappa* receptors, which create sedation; and the *delta*, which mediate depression, hallucination, and respiratory stimulation.[7]

Endorphins and opiate receptors in the body, however, are only part of the story of how we experience pleasure. A naturally occurring brain chemical, called dopamine, also plays a role. Dopamine performs multiple functions in the nervous system. In the basal ganglia of the brain, it works to create smooth, controlled movements. It is like a built-in "steadicam." People with Parkinson's disease, who suffer from trembling and lose the ability for controlled movements, are deficient in dopamine. Dopamine also functions as a pleasure chemical. If it is allowed to reach the frontal lobe, it can lessen pain or even produce euphoria. Pathways leading to the

---

6 J. Madeleine Nash, "Addicted: Why Do People Get Hooked? Mounting Evidence Points to a Powerful Brain Chemical Called Dopamine." *Time* 149, no. 18, May 5, 1997 (Internet archives).

7 "Nerves and Nervous Systems. Neuroactive Peptides," Britannica CD, Version 99 © 1994–1999, Encyclopædia Britannica, Inc.

frontal lobe control the amounts of dopamine that can reach it. Too much or too little can lead to serious imbalances.

Endorphins work with dopamine by opening up pathways for it. When the amount of endorphins inside the brain increases, the endorphins keep certain nerves inside the brain from blocking the flow of dopamine to the frontal lobe. As more dopamine reaches the frontal lobe, a person experiences pleasure. Some scientists are beginning to think that all pleasure-inducing drugs, including heroin, cocaine, and amphetamines, primarily affect the flow of dopamine to the brain. Like our endorphins, opioids and other drugs turn off dopamine inhibitors so that more dopamine reaches the parts of the brain that control emotions.

THE CHEMISTRY OF TOLERANCE, WITHDRAWAL, AND OVERDOSING

In some ways, the experience of heroin withdrawal is a cataclysmic return to many of the functions suppressed by opioid-receptor binding. A lot of the symptoms experienced by people in withdrawal are set off by activity in a part of the brainstem called the *locus coeruleus*, which is responsible for control of the body's fear-alarm system. This may explain the anxiety in addicts deprived of heroin.[8] Other phenomena, such as an increase in blood pressure, pupil dilation, diarrhea, anxiety, and increased respiration, seem like exact reversals of the opioid effect. They are symptoms of a suddenly activated sympathetic nervous system, which has been kept "asleep" by the constant use of opiates.

---

[8] A. Krivanek, "How Bad Is Heroin Withdrawal?" in *Heroin, Myths and Reality* (Boston: Allen & Unwin, 1988), (Internet excerpt).

Withdrawal from heroin cannot occur without the primary condition of tolerance to it. Opinions about the phenomenon of tolerance vary. Some researchers have maintained that it is a purely physiological state caused by alterations in the brain's drug receptors. But other experiments have shown that tolerance is environment-dependent. In laboratory experiments, animals who showed tolerance to repeated injections of opioids in one environment completely lost that tolerance when they moved to another environment.[9] This might indicate that tolerance is, at least in part, learned. However, tolerance also exhibits vivid physiological characteristics. For example, when an opiate antagonist, which is a drug that counteracts the effects of opiates, is administered to an opiate-tolerant person, that person immediately goes into painful withdrawal symptoms. If the same opiate antagonist is given to a person without an opiate addiction, he or she does not suffer such symptoms. Obviously, tolerance, whether learned or not, creates a special chemical state of affairs in an addict's body systems.

In some cases, tolerance may indirectly provide a clue as to why a person overdoses on heroin. Because of the increased number of heroin deaths throughout the country in the last few years, a new focus on the mechanism of heroin overdose has taken place. Researchers have a long way to go before they understand all the conditions that cause an overdose. They know that an overdose is a physical state in which some of the effects of the opiate are so powerful that body systems can't function: breathing, heartbeat, and several brain functions can slow to a dangerous

---

9 "Drugs and Drug Action. Opioid Analgesics," Britannica CD, Version 99 © 1994–1999, Encyclopædia Britannica, Inc.

level. The next stage is coma and perhaps death. However, they don't understand why the same body can tolerate certain amounts of opiate intoxication in some situations and less in others.

A classic case of overdose can occur during a relapse episode. If an addict used to taking a certain amount of heroin becomes abstinent, or even achieves a lowering of his or her customary dose, this will affect the tolerance level. Then, when the addict goes back to the old level of dosing, the body will react more powerfully to the drug than it did in the past. The addict may overdose and die.

Another classic scenario for heroin overdose is a sudden change in the nature of the drug supplied. The user may be basing doses on past experiences. Let's say that the heroin used in those experiences was customarily about 20 percent pure. Then, without warning, a new shipment begins to hit the streets. This shipment may be 60 percent pure. When the user injects or snorts or smokes the customary amount, he or she may overdose. Astonishingly, news of the overdose is likely to encourage rather than discourage other addicts. The news that some "pure shit" has hit the streets travels like wildfire, and an addict is practically willing to jump over the corpse of an overdosed friend to be the next in line to score.

In 1996, researchers published an article about fatal heroin overdose in the medical review *Addiction*.[10] Essentially, it challenged the widely held belief that most heroin-related deaths are the result of overdose of the drug. The researchers maintained that deaths involving only heroin were in the minority and that in most cases the presence of other depressants, such as alcohol and tranquilizers, played

---

[10] Shane Darke and Deborah Zador, "Fatal Heroin 'Overdose': A Review." *Addiction* 9, no. 12 (1996): 1765–1772.

Alcohol and tranquilizers are two depressants commonly abused by heroin addicts.

a role. The use of alcohol and tranquilizers is common among heroin users. Both drugs not only enhance the high, but they also smooth the process of coming down from it. And like heroin, these two drugs also depress the functioning of body systems.

WHAT ARE THE LONG-TERM
EFFECTS OF TAKING HEROIN?

We've already discussed the phenomena of tolerance and withdrawal among long-term opiate users. But there are many other long-term effects of heroin addiction. A large number of them are related not to the pharmacological properties of the drug itself, but to the conditions of taking it. In fact, heroin impurities, dirty needles, and unsanitary conditions, as well as the criminal environments of the drug abuse, constitute the majority of causes of long-term problems—not the heroin itself. Because of how and where heroin is taken, users are vulnerable to many lung, liver, skeletal, nerve, immune, and other diseases.

Let's start with the respiratory system. Long-term heroin users are at risk for pneumonias, lung abscesses, asthma, and lung fibroses. Some of these conditions are the result of inhaling irritating impurities when heroin is sniffed. Others are caused by the fact that any heroin use decreases the breathing rate and lung capacity over a period of time. This can eventually lead to respiratory diseases. Finally, some lung diseases are the result of heroin "culture." A lot of addicts smoke and consider cigarettes and their effect a part of the experience of getting high.

A higher proportion of heroin addicts suffer from liver complaints than do those in the general population. Several forms of viral hepatitis are common among addicts. This comes from needle-sharing, during which viral particles are moved from the bloodstream of one addict to another. But heroin addicts are also usually multi-substance abusers. Alcohol and various pharmaceuticals that may be taken to increase a high or ease a period of withdrawal all contribute to liver damage.

Bone and muscle damage is somewhat common among hardcore intravenous addicts. Some are plagued by osteomyelitis, a bone infection caused by bacteria or fungus, in their vertebrae. This probably comes from organisms injected into the body by the use of needles that are not sterile. Another common condition is myositis ossificans, or "drug-user's elbow." The disease is characterized by a calcified mass over a damaged muscle bundle caused by the clumsy use of needles.

Heroin users are likely to suffer from many neurological diseases. They may have trouble with their vision or even go blind due to a disease called toxic amblyopia, a disease of the optic nerve caused by a toxin. In the case of heroin users, that toxin is probably the quinine that is often used to cut street heroin. Bacterial infections from contaminated heroin can cause bacterial meningitis, brain abscesses, and other neurological diseases. Neurological disorders might also be the result of viral hepatitis or tetanus from infected needles.

Heroin addicts have many immune abnormalities. Researchers have yet to discover all of their origins. However, repeated injection of foreign, nonsterile substances into the bloodstream may be the cause of these conditions. What is more, heroin addicts who share needles are at extremely high risk for HIV infection.

There are a multitude of skin and vein problems among addicts who inject heroin. Abscesses, ulcerated sores, phlebitis, and other diseases caused by contaminated needles abound. So do collapsed veins. When a needle-using addict exploits the same vein over and over again, it eventually collapses. When the veins in the arm are used up, an addict will move to the legs, feet, genitals, or even the neck in the search for a new vein. Even if an intravenous heroin addict doesn't share needles, he or she is vulnerable to infection through use of the same needle over and over again, as it collects more and more bacteria from the environment.

Drug education programs have stressed clean needle programs. They've also encouraged addicts who cannot quit to sniff or smoke heroin rather than inject it. However, in the last few years, a new, somewhat mysterious illness has been diagnosed in addicts who smoke heroin.[11] The condition, called leukoencephalopathy, affects a person's motor skills. Two weeks after it is contracted, it leads to an increasing loss of muscle coordination. Users have slurred speech and a wobbling walk. To date, no one is absolutely certain about the ways in which smoking heroin can produce leukoencephalopathy, but some have posited that it decreases the supply of oxygen to brain tissue, causing that tissue to die.[12]

Perhaps the most grisly complication of injecting heroin is necrotizing fasciitis, or the flesh-eating bacteria disease. The disease begins as a painful skin infection and

[11] Christopher S. Wren, "Smoking Heroin Is Linked to Neurological Ailment," *New York Times*, December 1, 1996, Metropolitan Desk (Online Archives).

[12] Michael D. Hill, Perry W. Cooper, and James R. Perry, "Chasing the Dragon— Neurological Toxicity Associated with Inhalation of Heroin Vapour: Case Report." *Canadian Medical Association Journal* 162, no. 2 (2000): 236–238.

can eventually infect large areas of skin and flesh to the point of gangrene and lead to a general poisoning of body systems. It may only result in an extensive scar, but it may also lead to the loss of masses of flesh on an arm or a leg or even death. Heroin users aren't the only people who have come down with this relatively rare disease. However, the

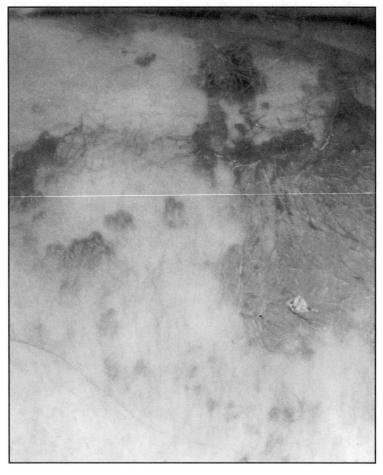

Necrotizing fasciitis.

use of heroin by injection seems to have a direct relationship to a greater chance of developing the disease.

What happens when a pregnant woman uses heroin? It is common knowledge among medical researchers that some of it is passed to the fetus through the placenta. A baby born to a heroin addict must withdraw from the drug in the first hours of life. Heroin-addicted babies may suffer from a variety of physical problems. However, no one is absolutely certain whether these problems are caused by heroin damage to the fetus during pregnancy or merely by the stress of withdrawing from heroin shortly after birth. Moreover, the heroin lifestyle among mothers often leads to poor prenatal care, influencing such factors as nutrition, rest, and the abuse of other substances. For whatever the reason, heroin-exposed babies have a higher incidence of infant death, low birth weight, and failure to thrive. [13]

WHAT ARE THE SOCIAL CONSEQUENCES OF HEROIN USE?

As already stated, a lot of the physical consequences of heroin use have to do with its social environment. For that reason, it is difficult to separate physical consequences from social consequences. Perhaps the following anecdote will serve as an example.

Marcy[14] was a twenty-seven-year-old heroin user who

---

[13] Hazel H. Szeto and Peter Y. Cheng, "Effects of Opiates on the Physiology of the Fetal Nervous System," in *Maternal Substance Abuse and the Developing Nervous System* (New York: Academic Press, 1992), pp. 215–234.

[14] Based on interview with "Marcy," a twenty-seven-year-old northern California heroin user. From the recorded transcript.

lived in Mendocino, California. She had sniffed heroin for five years, gone through one detox, and was abstinent for five months afterward. However, she says that the stress of her job as a graphic designer drove her back into snorting heroin after the five-month period. At first she confined her use of heroin to weekends and suffered no withdrawal symptoms. Nonetheless, after a few weeks, the one day began to extend into the entire weekend. When she woke up one Monday morning and had to call in sick to work due to withdrawal symptoms, she knew she was hooked again and began using once a day. She timed her habit so that she could get high after work. She went to bed high and woke up "straight" enough to get to work on time. Withdrawal symptoms didn't set in until late afternoon, and as long as no one asked her to work later than 4:30 P.M., she could get home in time for her dose.

The trouble began when a male co-worker began to notice the beginnings of her withdrawal symptoms in the parking lot. At first she thought it was the end of her job, but to her surprise, he approached her privately with the air of an insider. He, too, was a "chipper" (an occasional user), he explained. Perhaps it was the relief flooding through her that made her accept a date with him. It was only after they had slept together for the first time that she noticed the scars and bruises on his arms and legs. He was, he explained, a mainliner, not a snorter like her. This repulsed her at first, but she told herself that she was being judgmental. As the two became more intimate and began to do heroin together, she found herself getting curious about the mainlining experience. And after all, she thought, sniffing was "wasting" it, since it took so much more of the heroin to get high that way than it did by mainlining it.

Once Marcy began mainlining, she entered a new world of heroin addiction. She discovered that her lover had been hiding a much more serious addiction than he admitted to. He worked in production at her design company, and he timed his hours so that most of them fell within overtime. This gave him the opportunity to be alone in the office, a place where he shot up regularly. Marcy managed to change her schedule so that she'd be in the office late with him a couple days a week. There they shot up together. Marcy says that the "transgressive" feeling of doing heroin at work was fun at first. It was a way of working out her aggression about her job.

As Marcy's need for heroin increased, she naturally turned to her lover's suppliers. They weren't the petty San Francisco dealers she was used to but much larger "wheels." She was thrilled by the quality of the heroin they supplied and realized that what she was getting now was probably what her old dealers would obtain before they cut it and sold it to her. She didn't think about the connections of the big-time heroin dealers until one evening. Her boyfriend had just arrived at her home in the Mendocino hills for a night of partying, but no sooner had she let him in than a man pushed himself in after him. He was the strong-arm of one of the dealers. It seems that without telling Marcy, her boyfriend had accepted a large amount of heroin from the dealers and promised to sell it, but had used it up instead. Marcy thought back to the plentiful supply of heroin her boyfriend always had at the office. But now it was too late to think about where it must have come from. The strong-arm wanted to teach the boyfriend a lesson. He didn't want to maim him because that might prevent the boyfriend from being able to get together money.

So he pulled out a gun and handcuffed the couple to a chair. Once they were restrained, he sexually abused Marcy. Then he took out a pen-knife and severed one of the tendons in her thigh. To this day, Marcy walks with a limp. But that is not the end of the story. Marcy's anguish over the event didn't cause her to go to the police or even to break up with her boyfriend. They fought about what had happened, and eventually he worked things out with the dealers by agreeing to deal more for them. Meanwhile, Marcy, in flight from the mess she seemed to have gotten herself into, began to up her doses of heroin. She quit her job and began handling some of her boyfriend's deals. One blurry day, she was too clumsy while giving herself an injection. The tip of the needle broke off in a vein, an accident that is not uncommon among intravenous drug users. When Marcy went to the hospital, she was told there was danger of the broken piece of metal moving through the vein into her heart and damaging cardiac tissue, so she had to have surgery to have it removed. Afterward, she went into a six-month residential drug treatment facility. That was four years ago. She is still clean today.

Out of the several interviews with addicts I have conducted, I chose Marcy's story partly because of the fact that she comes from a middle-class professional environment. I wanted to show how powerful the social ramifications of heroin use can be. Marcy had had no experience with criminal or violent people. But suddenly she found herself at the mercy of one of them, after which she was hindered by physical problems and found herself living outside the legitimate working world. Of course, Marcy's story is overshadowed by the thousands of stories about addicts who developed their habits in the context of poverty. But in this context, violence, job loss, and cataclysmic medical occurrences are more expected. Still, all it took was long-term use to bring Marcy up to their level of trouble and heartache. Heroin is a great equalizer.

On the other hand, there is anecdotal evidence that even some heavy opiate users—for example, addicted physicians with access to morphine—manage to lead reasonably functional lives without ever going into recovery. Their drug-taking is protected from the usual social atmosphere of recreational drugs, such as street violence, contaminated substances, or poor access to health care. However, the long-term functional opiate addict represents only a tiny, isolated minority of cases. In general, because heroin is illegal, its use occurs amidst secrecy, lawlessness, and poor health standards. If the physiological risks of the drug don't bring the user down, eventually the social risks probably will.

A WORD TO THE WISE

What you have read about heroin so far in this book has been an attempt to portray the drug on several levels. There is the personal experience of using heroin. Then there are attempts to explain this process in scientific terms. Finally, there are the medical and sociological consequences of using heroin. Taken together, they represent the heroin experience in its entirety. However, heroin's lure, its kingdom of dreams and dangers, can never be fully and objectively described. For years, the dangers of this drug have been detailed by the media, outlined by the literature of drug awareness programs and taught in schools and universities. Yet again and again, some seem to be willing to flout all these risks for the heroin experience.

As you may have noticed, this book makes no attempt to sermonize. Any book that preaches can have little effect on those who are interested in what heroin really is. This is because no sermon can deny the intense euphoria experienced by some users. Opiates have been, and probably always will be, used for a variety of purposes. Their medical applications are well documented, but the dangerous experiments with them perpetrated by thrill-seekers, bohemian artists, rebellious musicians, or people looking for an escape from poverty or violence can't be interpreted so easily. What is more, it's becoming more and more obvious to drug counselors and drug researchers that some heroin use is a form of self-medication. In fact, in the past, before the invention of tranquilizers and antidepressants, opiates were the most widely used form of psychotropic treatment. They were used for depression, anxiety, and other mental illnesses. And even in the recent past, some respected researchers have studied the lives of patients on methadone programs and come up with some surprising hypotheses. Methadone is an opiate given to addicts to maintain and control their addiction to heroin. Some of the researchers who have studied people on methadone have come to the conclusion that opiates might effectively also be used as long-term psychotropic medications.[15] In other words, they feel that long-term, controlled opiate use might be desirable for some people with mental problems.

Yet, no hypothesis about the benefits of opiate use and no romantic tale of heroin use can take away the frighten-

---

[15] Gerald J. McKena, "Methadone and Opiate Drugs: Psychotropic Effect and Self-medication," *Annals of New York Academy of Science*, 398 (1982): 44–53.

ing consequences and risks involved in that pursuit. And no one can develop an informed opinion about heroin use without taking in the whole picture. That is why the next chapter will try to describe the world of heroin as it exists in the United States today. It is a frightening picture. For various reasons, heroin use has become an increasingly urgent social and medical problem in this country.

Chapter 2

The World of Heroin

What's the least likely place to encounter heroin abuse in America? Well, rural America isn't exactly the first thing that comes to mind when one thinks of heroin problems. Nevertheless, these days in America, even the remote countryside has been coming up with arrests associated with the drug. As an example, take Somerset County, Maryland. Population: 23,440.[16] In September 2000, Somerset County police in unmarked cars watched a group of five teenagers standing around a car at an Amoco One Stop in the town of Chance, talking about drugs. A search of their car yielded five bags of suspected heroin, some marijuana

•

[16] Somerset County Government web site:
http://www.mdarchives.state.md.us/msa/mdmanual/36loc/so/html/so.html

Even rural areas are subject to the problems caused by heroin.

and a scale. The police charged a twenty-year-old and a nineteen-year-old with possession and also arrested two seventeen-year-olds whom they later released to their parents. Drug use has doubled in the county in recent years, according to the State Department of Mental Health and Hygiene.[17]

That's what's happening in rural Maryland, but what's happening around the rest of the country? At the National Institutes of Health's Community Epidemiology Work Group (CEWG) annual meeting in 1999, drug abuse highlights for the country were presented. Heroin use figures were either stable or increasing in most cities. Seven large

[17] Michael Schaefer, "Police Look at Rural Heroin," *The Daily Times*, (Maryland) August 24, 2000.

Heroin Price and Purity

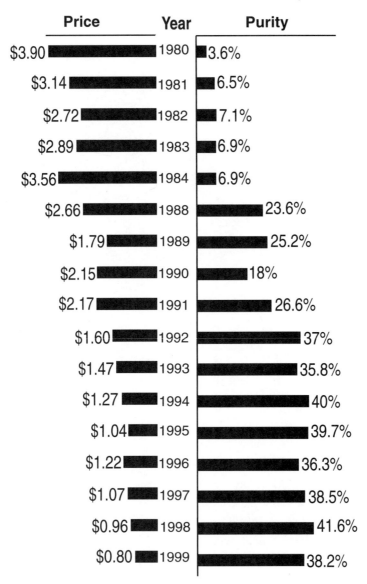

Price	Year	Purity
$3.90	1980	3.6%
$3.14	1981	6.5%
$2.72	1982	7.1%
$2.89	1983	6.9%
$3.56	1984	6.9%
$2.66	1988	23.6%
$1.79	1989	25.2%
$2.15	1990	18%
$2.17	1991	26.6%
$1.60	1992	37%
$1.47	1993	35.8%
$1.27	1994	40%
$1.04	1995	39.7%
$1.22	1996	36.3%
$1.07	1997	38.5%
$0.96	1998	41.6%
$0.80	1999	38.2%

Source: DEA Domestic Monitor Program

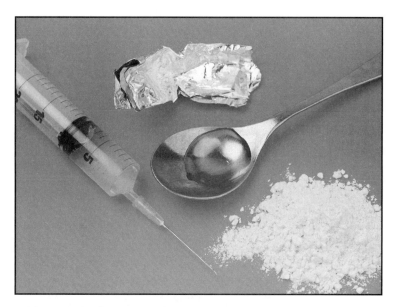

White powder heroin, and equipment used to prepare and inject it.

cities reported increases in heroin use among younger people.[18]

In their discussion of contemporary heroin use, the researchers for CEWG were careful to distinguish between two main types of heroin: Mexican "black tar" heroin, which is prevalent in the West and Southwest, and white powder heroin, from Colombia, Southeast Asia and Southwest Asia, which is more prevalent on the east coast. A third, less prevalent type, "brown heroin" is used in some places west of the Mississippi. Brown heroin also comes from Mexico. These types of heroin differ in mode of use. For example, black tar heroin has to be dissolved and

[18] "Community Epidemiology Work Group," Epidemiological Trends in Drug Abuse: Advance Report, December 1999" (Washington, D.C.: National Institutes of Health, National Institute on Drug Abuse, 1999).

diluted before it is injected. White powder heroin can be dissolved and injected but it also is snorted or smoked. It used to be highly cut and was considered inferior to black tar heroin, but it has been getting much purer in recent years. This increased strength makes it more possible to get the desired effects just by snorting or smoking. It also means that because of white powder heroin's increased purity, injection of it is more likely to lead to overdose. White powder heroin seems to attract younger people, possibly because of its versatility of use.[19]

In line with the types of heroin available in different parts of the country, researchers have found that the vast majority of users on the west coast inject the drug, probably because black tar heroin can't be snorted. On the east coast, many still inject, but a significant portion, as many as 74 percent, prefer to sniff or smoke. Meanwhile, two other trends were noted: a growing propensity to combine heroin with other drugs, especially alcohol and cocaine, and an increase in heroin-related deaths in many cities.[20]

In general, the typical heroin user consumes more heroin than he or she did a decade ago, probably because the purity of the dose is higher and the drug is getting purer.[21] In 1999, the National Household Survey on Drug Abuse (NHSDA) reported that there were approximately 149,000 new heroin users in the previous year. Nearly 80 percent of them were under the age of twenty-six.[22] During the 1990s,

[19] Community Epidemiology Work Group.

[20] Community Epidemiology Work Group.

[21] "Drugs of Concern: Heroin." Drug Enforcement Administration (DEA) on the Internet, home page: http://www.dea.gov/concern/heroin.htm

[22] "Drugs of Concern: Heroin."

use among teenagers in the eighth, tenth, and twelfth grades rose significantly.[23]

Certain cities showed striking new trends in the details of heroin use. In Atlanta, heroin sniffing is becoming more widespread among the young. In Baltimore, heroin use is also increasing among young people, especially in the suburban counties that surround the city. Sniffing heroin has increased among high school students in Boston. In St. Louis, high-purity heroin has led to a sudden comeback in use of the drug after several years of decline. San Diego showed higher incidences of adolescent heroin use, especially in the north county area. Heroin deaths have been rising in some cities, such as Baltimore, St. Louis, and Washington, D.C. In Colorado, in 1998, there were 135 heroin or opiate-related deaths. In Seattle, heroin deaths reached an all-time high in 1998. In Chicago, "speedballing"—using heroin with cocaine—has increased. And in Boston, 80 percent of heroin-related deaths were connected to the use of multiple substances, especially cocaine.[24] The use of multiple substances may be encouraged by dealers. For example, certain dealers in the Bronx borough of New York City have begun selling "piggy-back" combinations that consist of a $10 bag of heroin attached to a $10 bag of crack. And in Phoenix, dealers call a crack-and-black-tar-heroin combination "crack and black."[25]

In some areas of the country, the incidences of heroin use now seem to have surpassed that of cocaine. Throughout Massachusetts, heroin use has become the premier drug

---

[23] Community Epidemiology Work Group,"Epidemiological Trends in Drug Abuse: Advance Report, December 1999."(Washington, D.C.: National Institutes of Health, National Institute on Drug Abuse, 1999).

[24] Community Epidemiology Work Group.

[25] Community Epidemiology Work Group.

of choice among abusers, a situation that has not existed for more than ten years. The state's Department of Public Health has had to add 135 new beds to its network of drug treatment centers. This may be due in part to the cheapness and availability of the drug. In the year 2000, the average price for heroin in Massachusetts was about $4 a bag, less than your average six-pack. This makes it a favorite among younger people. They aren't put off by heroin's image either. The sleazy image of the strung-out addict feared by former generations has been replaced by something that seems less exotic and "cooler."[26]

The new higher purity of heroin presents a conundrum for drug enforcement officials. In September 2000, White House drug czar Barry McCaffrey[27] called attention to the entire region of New England, maintaining that heroin smuggled into the area by way of Canada was so pure that it had attracted a whole population of new heroin sniffers who might not have ever used the drug if they'd had to use needles. The new purer heroin can be snorted, and even eaten, to produce a high. However, cracking down on imports of purer heroin could lead to another crisis. If dealers have less of the substance, they are bound to cut it. Those already hooked on the drug will be driven to become intravenous users to get the best use of the product. And intravenous use introduces a whole new set of health problems, including serious bacterial infections, all forms of hepatitis, and AIDS.

---

[26] Kay Lazar, "Heroin Tops Coke on Mass Streets," *The Boston Herald*, June 18, 2000.

[27] Lisa Lipman, Associated Press, "Drug Czar Says High-purity Heroin a Threat to New England," *Boston Globe*, July 18, 2000.

Barry McCaffrey, White House drug czar who spoke out against the dangers New England faces from heroin smuggled in from Canada.

For regular heroin users, the path of life is often controlled by changes in drug supply. Peter is a seventeen-year-old senior high school student from New Haven, Connecticut. Both his parents are type-A professionals who are highly invested in their jobs. Peter and his younger sister grew up as "latchkey kids"—children who come home from school before their parents are home and sometimes have to fend for themselves for a few hours every day.

When Peter began sniffing white powder heroin in New Haven at the age of fifteen, no one at home even noticed. He would hide his pinpoint pupils with sunglasses that sometimes prompted his dad to make quips about "my son the jazz musician." On more than one occasion, he hid his withdrawal symptoms by claiming to have the flu, then

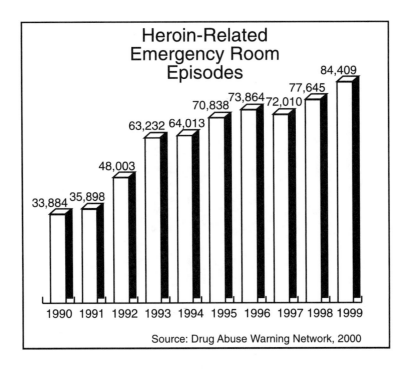

**Heroin-Related
Emergency Room
Episodes**

84,409

77,645

73,864 72,010

70,838

63,232 64,013

48,003

33,884 35,898

1990 1991 1992 1993 1994 1995 1996 1997 1998 1999

Source: Drug Abuse Warning Network, 2000

sneaked out to cop after his parents left for work. Because Peter snorted rather than shot heroin, he fooled himself into thinking that his habit wasn't serious, even though lots of people have developed tolerance and a full addiction to heroin by taking it intranasally. It is also possible to overdose by sniffing heroin.

Things remained as they were until Peter's father was told he was being transferred to another branch of the company in San Diego. It had never occurred to Peter what he would do if he lost his local sources for dope. At seventeen, Peter is now a west coast intravenous heroin user. Soon after arriving in San Diego, he discovered that the only heroin available was the black tar kind, which can't be snorted. Because he never shares needles, Peter doesn't think he has caught AIDS or hepatitis. But he's worried about an injection site on his arm that is not healing and is getting painful.

The increasing number of articles about heroin appearing in newspapers in large cities and small towns share a concern about the changing demographics of heroin. It is becoming more and more obvious that heroin users are getting younger and more middle class. When the drug tended to be confined to more marginal populations—ghetto minorities, members of the underclass, and bohemians—it produced reactions of repulsion or fear among the middle class. But it wasn't a community issue for them. Heroin users were remote macabre figures, curiously unaware of simple hygiene and the basic rules of decency. It's true that the many crimes committed by impoverished addicts who needed money to feed their habits brought attention to the crisis of heroin in America in the 1960s and 1970s, but the heroin culture in those years was thought to be distinctly urban.

Now that the middle class has heroin sitting in their laps, so to speak, journalists and politicians are looking at it in a more detailed—and more concerned—way. It's becoming obvious to them that heroin now represents a danger to young people of all income groups and cultural groups. "There is a whole new flock of young people out there who think they're reinventing the wheel, when, in fact, they're just one of the spokes," says the Reverend Charles Carnahan,[28] the executive director of AIDS Project Worcester in Massachusetts. What he means is that young people from a generation and class unfamiliar with the ravages of drug

---

[28] George B. Griffin, "Heroin Addicts Getting Younger." *Worcester Telegram & Gazette*, August 20, 2000.

abuse are currently looking at heroin as a novelty, without much knowledge of the consequences. Proof of this change can be found at Spectrum Health Systems health treatment centers in central Massachusetts. At these facilities, the median age of those seeking treatment for heroin addiction seems to have gone down. In the past, most were in their late twenties and early thirties, but now many are in their mid-twenties.[29] In Milwaukee County, Michigan, there were already fifteen heroin-related deaths by September 2000, compared to only twelve heroin-related deaths for the entire previous year. Four of the victims were from the suburbs. Nine were white, and some had full-time jobs.[30] Although these figures may not yet represent a suburban epidemic of substantial size, such deaths in these communities were virtually unknown until recently.

In April 2000, an article appeared in the *New York Times* entitled "Face of Heroin: It's Younger and Suburban; Cheaper Versions Reach Youths Who Haven't Seen the Drug's Damage."[31] The article opened with a mini-portrait of a high school varsity football player who would wait for his opportunity to sneak off for a snort. Although the article did not present teenage heroin use as an epidemic, it warned that the average age of first-time heroin users has been dropping for the last ten years. Heroin's popularity, the article claimed, was shifting from the inner city to the

[29] Griffin, "Heroin Addicts Getting Younger."

[30] "The Dangerous New Heroin," *Milwaukee Journal Sentinel*, August 21, 2000.

[31] Christopher S. Wren, "Face of Heroin: It's Younger and Suburban; Cheaper Versions Reach Youths Who Haven't Seen the Drug's Damage," *New York Times*, Metropolitan Desk, April 25, 2000.

Kurt Cobain, lead singer of the band Nirvana.

suburbs, although suburban teenagers are still more likely to use alcohol and marijuana than heroin. The article was careful not to write off the reasons for heroin use to that facile formula of "heroin chic" so often mentioned in the media. "Although popular culture has been blamed for making heroin look glamorous to adolescents," wrote the author, "drug treatment specialists call such an explanation simplistic; most of the recent initiates were still children in 1994, when Kurt Cobain, the lead singer of Nirvana, killed himself after struggling with heroin addiction." The main culprit leading young people to addiction, according to the article, wasn't media hype or the lives of faraway rock stars, but peer pressure, as well as depression, problems of self-esteem, and a need for acceptance. Some of the teenagers who are now addicts had merely slipped into heroin use casually, almost accidentally, finding it for sale at raves, where they were used to buying and taking Ecstasy. These teenagers are more likely to be attracted to heroin than their peers from poor urban communities, many of whom have already seen the damage it could do to family and friends. The image of the "pusher" has also changed. Rather than being a seedy adult who hangs out in school yards trying to corrupt the young, a dealer tends to be a fellow schoolmate, who might even be younger than the user.

There is one striking discrepancy in this new focus on middle-class suburban heroin addiction. In general, drug addiction is still more common in urban settings of poverty than it is among the middle class. The new militancy that has sprung up in reaction to the threat of suburban heroin seems shallow in light of the fact that not as many vocal opponents of heroin seemed to care when heroin was devastating the inner city. Those poor communities constantly witness true epidemics of recreational drugs. Drug abuse in the ghetto is a much more severe problem than it is in the suburbs. Did such a situation ever receive sufficient attention?

THE POST-BEAT GENERATION

The suburban heroin problem seems symptomatic of deeper social and psychological problems. These problems are only briefly touched upon in most media analyses, but it seems obvious that heroin use in the suburbs is no mere fashion trend. Complicated feelings of depression and nihilism in suburban communities may be fueling it. The psychedelic experimentations of the 1960s and 1970s were also a largely middle-class phenomenon, but they had a more celebratory character, despite eventual negative consequences. In contrast, the new heroin culture of the suburbs seems to be a culture of despair, not celebration, embodied by the nihilistic Grunge lyrics of a Nirvana or Smashing Pumpkins song. Heroin addiction in the suburbs is deeply related to other phenomena of alienation in the same community. It is, in a way, a new version of "Beat" culture.

The term "Beat," as it was loosely defined in the 1950s to describe a "beat generation" of "hipsters," referred not only to the beat of jazz but to feelings of hopelessness and ineffectuality experienced by young intellectuals in the face of the Cold War, the atom bomb, and the new conformity of 1950s society. They felt that the world around them had them "beat," and they were attracted to somber existential feelings about the disappearance of meaning in life and the "death of God." The world of the Beats, epitomized by writers like Jack Kerouac, Allen Ginsberg, and William Burroughs, and iconoclastic jazz musicians like Thelonius Monk and Miles Davis, was also a heroin-infused world. One of the best memoirs about the Beat sensibility and its connection to heroin abuse is *The Basketball Diaries*, written after the Beat generation by Baby Boomer Jim Carroll. It is the story of a teenager growing up on Manhattan's Lower East Side and falling into heroin addiction and petty crime. It's a book of dark beauty—poetic, pessimistic, and adolescent. The movie version of *The Basketball Diaries* was cited by the media in connection with the shooting spree that

Beatnik writer and poet Jack Kerouac.

occurred at Columbine High School in Littleton, Colorado in 1999. Apparently, those responsible for the shootings had seen the film *The Basketball Diaries* and were "inspired" by the fantasy sequence in which the character played by Leonardo DiCaprio, dressed in a black trench coat, kills students in the hallway of his school. Although that scene isn't in the book, both film and book are statements of teenage alienation and desperation.

The Basketball Diaries was written decades ago, yet its adolescent angst matches an element of today's suburban malaise. And just as heroin becomes a desperate antidote to that malaise in the book, it is playing the same role for today's alienated suburban teenagers.

What is there about American suburban life that has caused this sudden, self-destructive revolt among a small minority? Perhaps it is suburbia's failure to provide less of an outlet for nonconformist ideas and feelings than there was in the past. Teenagers in the 1950s, 1960s and 1970s had codes of rebellion and nonconformity. The juvenile delinquent in his black leather jacket and motorcycle and the bearded "beatnik" or the pot-smoking hippies were all symbolic of youthful middle-class alienation. The lifestyles they entailed led to complications, but in many cases, there was a way back from extreme situations. Those images are hackneyed now, and no dynamic symbols of alienation have replaced them. In the

The ripped jeans and long hair of this hippie symbolized the rebellion and nonconformity of the 1960s.

suburban world of shopping malls, three-car families and at-home media entertainment, everything is beginning to seem inescapably uniform. There are few opportunities to express meaningful rebellion. At best, adolescent middle-class alienation today has a passive quality, a post-Grunge sense of defeat and apathy that is a prime motivator for heroin abuse.

THE NORTHWEST HEROIN PROBLEM

Heroin may be tainting the suburbs, but in northwestern cities it has reached epidemic proportions. Both Seattle and Portland are on a heroin smuggling route running all the way from Mexico to Canada. They are also international ports, which attract black tar heroin smugglers coming from Mexico and South America.[32] Use of the drug has sky-rocketed in the Pacific Northwest. In the Portland area, heroin overdose deaths among young and middle-aged men are nearly as prevalent as deaths from cancer or heart disease. And heroin overdose deaths in this city have been climbing steadily since 1993.

Seattle faces a similar situation. From 1990 to 1999 it experienced a 134-percent rise in heroin overdose deaths. A wide majority of the victims were male.[33] As in most areas of the Northwest, heroin addicts use the drug intravenously, since it is of the black tar variety. A lot of the deaths are probably due to a pattern in which the user stops injecting

---

[32] Luis Cabrera, Associated Press, "Heroin Overdose Deaths Rising Fast in Northwest, Study Shows," *San Diego Union Tribune*, July 24, 2000.

[33] Associated Press, "Cheap Heroin Laying Waste to Men in Northwestern Cities," *San Francisco Chronicle*, July 21, 2000.

for a period of time, either because he is in jail, has run out of money, or is in rehabilitation. Then he goes back to it, often injecting the same dose. Tolerance has declined, however, and so overdose results.[34] But, in general, hardcore addicts aren't put off by overdoses. On the contrary, news of an overdose can unleash a rush to get the drug. The addicts feel they can judge the correct dose, and their goal is to obtain the purest that they can find.

Seattle has an estimated 15,000 to 20,000 addicts. Seattle's heroin sells for about $20 a dose and is very potent. Sometimes those who want to stop shooting have to wait more than a year to start treatment.[35] In 1999, King County, in which Seattle resides, had only 1,750 slots available for treatment despite the tens of thousands of local addicts who might have needed to go into recovery.[36]

As early as 1997, a federal study of emergency-room admissions identified Seattle as one of the top cities for heroin-related problems, along with Baltimore, Newark, and San Francisco. According to Henry Ziegler, head of the prevention division of the Seattle–King County Public Health Department, the documented heroin overdoses are only "the tip of the iceberg." Heroin deaths now seem to run through a cross-section of the community, probably across many age and socioeconomic groups.[37]

---

[34] Associated Press, "Cheap Heroin Laying Waste to Men in Northwestern Cities."

[35] Cabrera, "Heroin Overdose Deaths Rising Fast in Northwest, Study Shows."

[36] Sam Howe Verhovek, "Record Number of Heroin Deaths Casts Shadow Over Seattle," *New York Times*, National Desk, January 21, 1999.

[37] Verhovek, "Record Number of Heroin Deaths Casts Shadow Over Seattle."

Seattle, Washington, has a high population of heroin addicts.

Of course, the 1994 suicide of Kurt Cobain, of rock group Nirvana fame, and subsequent confessions about heroin use by Courtney Love, his wife and member of the rock group Hole, only increased Seattle's reputation as a center for heroin abuse. Some people believe the Grunge image has attracted people interested in heroin and contributed to the epidemic, though this belief is not supported by any statistical research.

Buckles is a twenty-six-year-old former heroin addict who was raised in the Seattle area and was a hardcore Nirvana fan in the early 1990s. His parents are separated. As a teenager, he lived in a Seattle suburb with his mother but spent weekends in the city with his father as part of their divorce agreement. His father was severely depressed by the divorce and spent

HEROIN SLANG*	
Banging	Injecting heroin
Boy	Heroin
Chasing the dragon	Smoking heroin
China white	Powder white heroin from Asia
Chiva	Heroin (Spanish word for a young goat)
Cooking	Heating heroin to dissolve it for injection
H-bomb	Ecstasy cut with heroin
Hit	Dose
Junk	Heroin
Lady	Heroin
Mainlining	Intravenous injection
Mexican mud	Brown heroin
Nod out	Losing consciousness for a few seconds on heroin
Rig	Syringe
Smack	Heroin
Skin-popping	Injecting heroin under the skin rather than in a vein
Spike	Needle
Tar baby	West coast teenage heroin user
Works	Heroin paraphernalia (needles, spoons, tourniquets, etc.)

* Andrew Backover, Marisa Taylor, and Karen Brooks, "The Hell of Heroin," Star-Telegram Writers. Chart: "Heroin Slang," *The Fort Worth Star-Telegram,* March 22, 1998.

most of the weekend sleeping. Buckles therefore had to make his own meals and find his own way to amuse himself. It was also around this time—at sixteen—that he decided he was gay. He began having an affair with a boy in his father's neighborhood who took him to a Nirvana concert and to several raves. The two enjoyed doing Ecstasy together and having sex, but after a few months the friend started experimenting with heroin. "I didn't want to lose the guy," says Buckles. "I needed his company and I was afraid the heroin would take him away from me. So I started doing it with him."

As it turned out, he did lose his friend. The friend's parents sent him to rehab, and Buckles was left to sort out his addiction himself. Eventually, he told his father about the problem, who "came to," as Buckles puts it, and sent his son to rehab. When Buckles got out of rehab, he found that his father was much more available to him. The two formed a close bond that soon enabled Buckles to discuss his homosexuality with his father. His father could accept it, which Buckles says was a great motivator to full recovery. He now goes to college part-time and works part-time as a web designer. He's still living with his dad but is thinking of leaving to move in with his new boyfriend.

OPIATE ADDICTS: THE FAMOUS AND NOT SO FAMOUS

Throughout the twentieth century and into the twenty-first, the myth of heroin, in all its images—as a poetic myth, as a social problem, and as a medical problem—has permeated American culture. Like a chameleon, opiates change their appearance over and over again. The image of heroin has been manipulated by the creative people who were addicted to it and by changing cultural requirements. From the jazz culture of heroin that began in the 1920s to the heroin chic looks of the fashion photography of the late 1990s, the image of heroin has undergone multiple transformations. What follows are descriptions of the lives of just a few newsworthy people whose lives were deeply challenged by the heroin or opiate experience.

Hubert Selby, Jr., Novelist. Born in Brooklyn in 1928 to a poor family, Selby was a merchant sailor by the time he was a teenager. However, he soon fell seriously ill from a nearly fatal lung disease and spent approximately ten years in hospitals. He survived and recovered, but uncontrollable anger over what he'd endured led him to alcoholism and heroin addiction. It also inspired him to write. His 1964 novel *Last Exit to Brooklyn*, which describes the miserable lives of the inhabitants of a poor Brooklyn neighborhood, catapulted him to fame. However, his addiction problems led to a stint in prison, part of which was spent in solitary confinement. This produced a frightening account of the experience in a new novel, *The Room* (1971).

By the time a film was made from *Last Exit to Brooklyn* in 1990, Selby had been in recovery for more than a decade. He now lives, teaches, and writes drug-free in California and considers his path to recovery and its spiritual and psychological ramifications the greatest experience of his life.

Janis Joplin, Singer. A late 1960s and early 1970s culture heroine for millions of Baby Boomers, Janice Joplin stunned the music world with her gravelly blues voice, unstructured, intuitive singing, and wild life style. For many members of the "Love Generation," her talent, her opinions, and her lesbian love affairs represented the full flowering of 1960s culture. However, she never overcame her resentment and sense of exclusion from the small Florida suburban community where she grew up.

Rock singer Janis Joplin.

Throughout her career as one of the most talented singers of her generation, she maintained regular contact with her middle-class family while simultaneously leading her bohemian life style of free love, drug experimentation, and rock improvisation. Her energy seemed limitless, and her drive to realize herself as a singer was relentless. On October 4, 1970, she died of an overdose of heroin in Los Angeles.

William Henry Welch, Physician.[38] Born in 1852, Welch was one of the founders of the Johns Hopkins Medical School. A respected surgeon and a member of a distinguished New York family, he was a graduate of Yale, where he had been captain of the football team.

Welch was one of the first American medical researchers to experiment with cocaine as a local anesthetic for surgery. During this period of experimentation, he himself became addicted to it, and his problems in dealing with this addiction began to interfere with his practice. He dropped out of sight to try to cure his addiction and returned years later to enjoy a stable career as a doctor. During this time, he helped develop a technique of antisepsis, which was a way of keeping germs out of wounds during operations. He continued to have a noteworthy career as a skillful surgeon until his death in 1922. Only after his death was it discovered that he had traded cocaine addiction for a long-term morphine addiction and had practiced his profession of surgeon during this entire period.

Billie Holiday, Singer. Born on April 7, 1915, in Philadelphia, Billie Holiday was the illegitimate daughter of

---

[38] Edward M. Brecher and the Editors of *Consumer Reports Magazine,* "Some Eminent Narcotics Addicts," *The Consumers Union Report on Licit and Illicit Drugs, Consumer Reports Magazine,* 1972.

a black domestic worker. Her father, Clarence Holiday, played guitar with Fletcher Henderson. Starting out in the jazz clubs of Harlem, Holiday was discovered by John Hammond, who arranged for her to record with Benny Goodman in 1933. She went on to sing with Dizzy Gillespie, Artie Shaw, and other jazz greats. Her style was an updated, more modern version of Bessie Smith's blues singing style. A song Holiday wrote after the traumatic citing of a Southern lynching, "Strange Fruit," is a jazz standard today.

Holiday performed all over the world. However, her growing heroin addiction led to increasing legal and medical problems. After an arrest for possession of heroin, she spent most of 1947 in prison.

Legal problems with heroin also caused her to lose her cabaret license in New York, and she was banned from performing there for a period of time. By the 1950s, her voice had taken on a darker, more expressionistic character, partly due to physical health problems and depression. It also had a slurred quality that may have been symptomatic of a heroin high. But she retained her power to thrill audiences until her death at the age of 44 in 1959, caused partly by addiction.

Loren Walgreen, Mother.[39]   Loren Walgreen was the wife of Tad Walgreen, the son of Walgreen Co.'s retired chief executive, Cork Walgreen. Tad met Loren in 1988 when both were in a rehab program. He died at the age of thirty-six of a cocaine overdose in the late 1990s. However, in 1996, before Tad died, Loren and he had become

---

[39] Martha Irvine, Associated Press, "The Walgreens' War, Second Drug Death Finishes Family," *Houston Chronicle*, December 21, 1999.

involved in an ugly custody battle for their two children initiated by Tad's father and stepmother. The chief executive wanted their two children because he felt Tad and Loren were unfit parents. There was testimony that the couple were living in filth with a hole punched in their wall. Although the elder Walgreens finally got custody of the children, they were never able to legally adopt them.

Meanwhile, deprived of her children, Loren sank further into addiction. After her husband's death, friends accused the Walgreens of abandoning her and worsening her problem by keeping her children from her. In 1999, at the age of thirty-one, she died in a basement apartment, victim of an apparent overdose.

Gia Carangi, Model. Known simply as "Gia," top model Gia Marie Carangi was born on January 29, 1960 and died at age twenty-six. She was one of the most sought-after models of the early 1980s, and her sultry looks graced the covers of several issues of *Vogue* magazine. Her life style of heroin use and her erratic behavior on shoots made her notorious in the world of fashion, but photographers continued to clamor for her because of her swarthy, sensual face and ability to project herself to the viewer. In 1986 she died of AIDS complications. It's likely that she contracted the HIV virus through the use of needles.

William Seward Burroughs, Writer. William Burroughs was born in 1914 in Kansas. His father was the inventor of the first mechanical adding machine. Burroughs was the black sheep of the family, drawn to literature and bohemian ways at an early age. In the 1950s, he was living in New York, nursing an addiction to heroin, and then began a writing career. His first book, *Junky*, published under the pen-name William Lee, is his most autobiographical work. It is also one of the most vivid descriptions

Gia Carangi, one of the best-known models of the 1980s.

of the heroin subculture of the time. With Allen Ginsberg, Burroughs became one of the most acclaimed writers of the Beat generation, especially after the publication of the novel *Naked Lunch*. The book is an electrifying hodge-podge of eccentric theories about addiction, surreal narratives about homosexuality, and stunning collages of word play. Today it is considered a classic of postmodern literature. Burroughs' addiction to heroin continued on and off during most of his eighty-three years. During his long years of addiction, he developed a philosophical and metaphysical theory of addiction that influenced his writing. He also advocated unusual cures for heroin addiction, such as the use of the compound apomorphine, an emetic derived from morphine. In the last decade of his life, he became an icon for certain alternative music cultures and transgressive writers. More than any other writer, his name comes up in discussions about the surge in popularity of heroin today. He died in 1997 in his hometown of Lawrence, Kansas.

Lonnie "Ted" Binion, Gambling Scion. Binion[40] was the son of Lester "Benny" Binion, the founder of the Horseshoe Casino, one of the most profitable gambling houses in the early days of Las Vegas. As a result, Ted was a millionaire worth about $50 million, who lived in a 6,200-square-foot home on Palomino Lane in one of Vegas's most upscale neighborhoods.

In 1998, at the age of fifty-five, Binion was discovered dead on the floor of his den. Next to him were an empty, open bottle of Xanax and a piece of slashed balloon that had probably contained black tar heroin. The day before, the millionaire had purchased twelve balloons of the drug, which he said was the best he had had in a long time. However, in 2000, two people, Sandy Murphy and her lover Rick Tabish, were convicted of killing Binion and planting the drugs near him in an attempt to steal his buried treasure of more than $5 million in silver.

Kurt Cobain, Singer-Musician. Cobain's career involvement with heroin and his death by suicide are probably the best-known heroin-related stories today. Cobain's band

---

[40] Michael Kaplan, "Good-bye, Mr. Chips. (Ted Binion's Death a Homicide)," *Los Angeles Magazine*, February 2000.

Nirvana was a leading light in the Grunge movement, which started in Seattle, and was just as much a life-style movement as a style of music.

Grunge was a reincarnation of the hippie ethos adapted for contemporary times, or, in a sense, a backlash to hippie culture, a kind of "metallic" version of it. The torn jeans, long hair, and plaid flannel shirts of Grunge culture were symbols of its followers' alienation from materialism. Like the hippie culture, the Grunge movement was a return to basics and represented a dissatisfaction with consumerism. It looked favorably at "indie" bands, low-tech music, and heartfelt, nakedly poetic lyrics. Grunge contained both punk and pop elements, but it also possessed an element of rural nostalgia. Cobain himself was born in Aberdeen, Washington, a small upstate logging town. At the age of eight, he was deeply troubled when his parents underwent a hostile separation. His songs spoke of early isolation from both family and community and they expressed a sense of ruined idealism that was morbid but full of aesthetic sensitivities. It was this sense of ruined idealism and hopelessness that led Cobain to heroin addiction, which eventually took his life.

In the months before his death, Cobain fled attempts at rehabilitation from multiple drug use and relapsed into taking heroin. Then, finally, on the morning of April 8, 1994, he was discovered by an electrician lying in a pool of blood in his home. He had shot himself two or three days before with a 12-gauge shotgun. He had left a suicide note. The news of Cobain's death paralyzed Seattle. His wife, Courtney Love, read his suicide note on national television. Millions of fans mourned. The event focused attention not only on Seattle and its drug abuse problems but also on the rising use of heroin among young people all over the country.

There are hundreds of other stories involving heroin abuse among celebrities. Nineteen-fifties rock singer Frankie Lymon, Rolling Stone guitarist Keith Richards, and Andy Warhol superstar Nico, who was also a member of the rock group The Velvet Underground, are just a few examples. But there are tens of thousands more stories of heroin abuse from every socioeconomic sector that aren't linked to noteworthy careers or unusual creativity. It may be true that creativity sometimes arises from neurotic personalities and highly sensitive individuals who find that their unusual imaginations are in conflict with society. It may also be true that some of these unusual people consequently become drug abusers. But it certainly is not true that everyone who becomes an abuser of heroin is creative. The vast majority of heroin users will never become celebrities; on the contrary, their addiction may prevent them from reaching even minimum levels of functioning. For the most part, heroin abuse today is an illness that permeates all of society, and not just the creative elite.

Did heroin always play the same role in society? Were the penalties for using it always the same? The next chapter presents a brief history of heroin and other opiates. You may be surprised to see how the image of heroin has changed over the decades.

Chapter 3

Heroin History:
Then and Now

Opiates, even heroin, were not always seen as a danger to society. In the past, they were viewed primarily as a means to relieve pain and soothe the mind. It was only later that opiates took on their demonic aspect and became associated with severe addiction and crime. For several thousand years before that, opium had been considered one of the most valued drugs of medicine. Raw opium was considered a miracle drug by early physicians, such as the Greek doctor Hippocrates.

Narcotics from the opium poppy have been used since ancient times to relieve pain and to provide a source of euphoria. The opium poppy was probably first discovered growing wild in the mountains bordering the eastern Mediterranean during the Neolithic Age.[41] During the

---

[41] Alfred McCoy with Cathleen B. Read, "Heroin: The History of a 'Miracle Drug,'" in *The Politics of Heroin in Southeast Asia* (New York: Harper & Row, 1972).

Neolithic Age opium use spread westward through Europe, and reached India and China in the first centuries of the first millennium after Christ. For three or four thousand years, opium remained one of the most valued drugs of medicine. There were many uses for opium, and many methods of ingestion. It was eaten, smoked, or drunk in a mixture of alcohol and opium, which was known as laudanum. From ancient Greek times until the early part of the twentieth century, opiates were freely prescribed for a vast variety of ailments in both the East and the West. During the eighteenth and nineteenth centuries in some western European countries, opium-based medicines were used for coughs, headaches, colds, painful menstrual complications, and other ills.

It wasn't until the first half of the nineteenth century that the active ingredients of opium were chemically isolated. The first of these ingredients was morphine, isolated in 1803 by the German pharmacist F.W.A. Sertüner. Shortly afterward, the milder narcotic, codeine, was isolated from morphine.

By the mid-nineteenth century, the invention of hypodermic needles opened the way for injection of morphine. In 1858, two American doctors began experimenting with injecting it directly into the bloodstream.[42] These advances greatly increased the efficacy of opiates as pain-killers, and soon their use in hospitals and by physicians became commonplace.

The English writer Thomas De Quincey drew attention to the problem of opiate addiction as early as the 1820s, in his essay, *Confessions of an Opium Eater*, but in general, the addictive qualities of opiates were not considered a widespread problem before the first or second decade of the

---

[42] McCoy and Read, "Heroin: The History of a Miracle Drug."

twentieth century. This does not mean that opiates weren't widely used by all segments of society in America and western Europe until then. They were easily and cheaply available over the counter in pharmacies and other stores as well as by mail order, and a large segment of the population used them. Scholars and researchers continue to debate why they were not considered a serious social problem. One factor, of course, is that there are fewer statistics available on opiate use in that period than there are on opiate use today. However, the most important reason may be that they were not illegal. Since their use was considered legitimate for a host of minor ailments, users never became part of the criminal network needed to become opiate users today. If they did develop habits, these habits were neither expensive nor illegal. Moreover, a person who claimed to use opiates for health reasons was not regarded in a judgmental manner.

There was yet another reason why opiates were not considered a problem—at least before the invention of injectable morphine: Eating, smoking, or drinking opium produces a milder high than injecting opiates. Development of injectable morphine proved to be a benchmark in the history of opiates, marking the beginning of a pronounced concern over the addictive potential of opiates. Several decades later, in the teens and twenties of the twentieth century, the first laws controlling opiate use would be instituted.

Physicians in the nineteenth century prescribed opiates for a surprisingly wide spectrum of ailments, including cough, diarrhea, dysentery, angina, insanity, tetanus, and vomiting during pregnancy. Opiates were also used as tranquilizers, since today's modern tranquilizers (such as Valium and Xanax) hadn't yet been invented. An even more surprising use of opium and morphine was as a treatment for alcoholism. Many late-nineteenth-century physicians believed that chronic morphine use was less dangerous to the abuser and to society than alcoholism. The amount of morphine needed to maintain a long-term addict cost less than the amount of alcohol purchased by an alcoholic. Also, the morphine seemed to calm the passions rather than stimulate them as alcohol did. Opiate use was less likely to produce violence and criminal behavior than alcohol was.[43] The use of opium, morphine, and codeine as a tranquilizer, as a treatment for alcoholism, and as a home remedy for dozens of complaints in the United States continued through the first third of the twentieth century. As late as the 1930s, some doctors in some states were still prescribing opiates as a long-term treatment for alcoholism.

The late nineteenth century saw a range of patent medicines containing opium or morphine. These included Ayer's Cherry Pectoral, for coughs; Godfrey's Cordial, a "cure-all" mixture of opium, molasses, and sassafras; and Mrs. Winslow's Soothing Syrup. Some opiate medicines were even used to allay the teething pains of infants.

In San Francisco, there were dozens of opium-smoking dens. Opium-smoking had been introduced into the West by the Chinese who arrived during the 1850s and 1880s to build the western railroads. Whereas the whites' use of opiates would go on virtually unchecked for several decades, the city of San Francisco took exception to its practice by immigrants. Once it was discovered that the "opium dens" where opium was smoked in the Oriental style included white women and men who smoked side by side with the Chinese, there was a widespread outcry. In 1857, San

---

[43] Edward M. Brecher and the Editors of Consumer Reports Magazine, "Opiates for Pain Relief, for Tranquilization and for Pleasure," *The Consumers Union Report on Licit and Illicit Drugs*, 1972.

Francisco adopted an ordinance prohibiting the smoking of opium in such places.[44]

In the nineteenth century, the majority of narcotics users were women.[45] This was probably because opiates were prescribed for a host of female-associated ailments, including menstrual problems, nausea or depression during pregnancy, and migraines. What is more, social drinking, especially outside the house, was frowned upon for women. So while husbands could consume large amounts of alcohol in public establishments, women seeking mind-altering experiences contented themselves with the use of opiates at home for their "ills." Thus, an 1878 survey of opiate users in Michigan found that over 60 percent were female. Also, nineteenth-century opiate users were older than today's heroin abusers. An 1880 Chicago survey showed that the average for both males and females was close to age forty. The gender and age of most opiate users, as well as the social image of the opiate user, would change abruptly after 1914, when the Harrison Narcotic Act would restrict the availability of opiates. Very quickly, the majority of opiate users would become male and involve a younger age, as opiate use would become an outlawed activity linked with criminal activity.[46]

In 1874, the English scientist Charles Alder Wright synthesized heroin (then known only as diacetylmorphine) for the first time by boiling morphine and acetic anhydride

---

44 "Opium Smoking Is Outlawed," in *The Consumers Union Report on Licit and Illicit Drugs*, 1972.

45 Edward M. Brecher and the Editors of Consumer Reports Magazine, "What Kinds of People Used Opiates?" *The Consumers Union Report on Licit and Illicit Drugs*, 1972.

46 Brecher et al., "What Kinds of People Used Opiates?"

over a stove.[47] After testing the drug, however, he abandoned his research. During the late 1880s, chemist David Dott and physician Ralph Stockman began to investigate the effects of diacetylmorphine in frogs and rabbits. They found that it was five to nine times as potent as morphine. In 1898, diacetylmorphine was produced by the Bayer Company under the auspices of the same research team that had produced aspirin. The researchers believed that it would make an extremely effective cough suppressant that would help people with severe lung diseases, such as bronchitis, asthma, and tuberculosis.[48] Thinking that the drug was a nonaddicting substitute for other opiates, the company decided to market the drug with the help of a massive marketing campaign. They named the drug "heroin," after the Greek term *heros*, which refers to an ancient Greek protagonist whose amazing deeds led him to be honored as a demigod. The substance was marketed as a miracle drug in several countries, and many doctors prescribed it as a supposedly nonaddicting medicine for coughs, headaches, and other ills. Syrups and cough drops containing heroin were widely used for more than a decade. It was only ten or twenty years later that the addiction potential of heroin became clear to physicians. It would take at least fifteen years of nonrestricted heroin use after 1898 until the medical community began to reevaluate the drug.

Use of opiates continued largely unabated into the first decade of the twentieth century. The initial step in the

---

[47] McCoy and Read, "Heroin: The History of a 'Miracle Drug.'"

[48] Walter Sneader, "The Discovery of Heroin," *The Lancet*, November 21, 1998.

control of the use of opiates came in 1906 when Congress passed the first Pure Food and Drug Act. The act required that medicines containing opiates list these ingredients on their labels. This encouraged educational campaigns against the indiscriminate use of opiates. However, those already addicted to opiates were not much affected by the law, since opiate-containing products were still widely available. It would take the Harrison Narcotic Act of 1914 to change the climate of opiate use in America.

For many years, the United States had criticized Britain for shipping opium grown in India to China. The practice had led to two "opium wars" between Britain and China in the nineteenth century. Not only were the British interfering with Chinese opium production and exports, but they were also increasing the addiction among the Chinese by shipping Indian opium to China. In 1909, President Theodore Roosevelt led the call for an international investigation of the opium problem. Several international conferences concerning the opium trade were held during the first decade of the twentieth century. Then, in 1912, at The Hague, the first international agreement concerning restrictions on the importation of opium was reached. This led to discussions among law-makers in the United States about the domestic regulation of opiates. Finally, in 1914 the Harrison Act[49] placed a special tax on all producers, importers, manufacturers, distributors and sellers of opium and coca leaves and products derived from them. It also required that those involved in these businesses had to be licensed to do so. Physicians were still allowed to prescribe opiates as they saw fit and were only required to keep records.

---

[49] "The Harrison Narcotic Act (1914)," in *The Consumers Union Report on Licit and Illicit Drugs*, 1972.

At first, the law was not interpreted as prohibitive of opiate use. But later certain clauses of the law allowed law enforcement officials to severely limit the perscription or sale of products containing opiates. For example, law enforcement officials eventually decided that opiates could not lawfully be prescribed by doctors to maintain an addiction since, at the time, addiction was not considered a legitimate illness.

Limiting the prescription of opiates quickly led to the criminalization of their use by addicts. In fact, the wrongful use of narcotics suddenly increased after the Harrison Act was implemented. Opiate sales shifted from pharmacies and mail order companies to the streets, and many addicts were forced to get their opiates from criminal sources. To stem the rising tide of illegal opiate use, Congress passed more severe laws in the 1920s. For example, in 1924, a law prohibiting all importation of heroin, even for medicinal use, was enacted. This was because, following passage of the Harrison Act, many addicts had converted from morphine or codeine to heroin. The new law was an attempt to stem the rising tide of opiate addiction by instituting harsher controls. However, the ban on heroin did not prevent the conversion from morphine to heroin among addicts. Instead, heroin replaced morphine almost completely on the black market.[50]

The rest of the story of opiates in America is well-known today. In the 1920s and 1930s, the number of illegal heroin addicts began to grow. The sharp decline in legally available opiates encouraged rather than ended the use of heroin, which was then a notoriously illegal opiate, closely

---

[50] "The Harrison Narcotic Act (1914)"

interwoven with crime and marginal populations. Criminal syndicates took over the heroin trade and proliferated its use in the black ghetto for profit. Production of heroin shifted from legal factories in Europe to secret laboratories in Shanghai and China.[51] Vast amounts of illegal heroin were shipped to European criminal syndicates and American Mafiosi. In Marseilles, France, Corsican criminal syndicates set up laboratories that produced heroin for export to European markets and the United States. Only the outbreak of World War II disrupted the international heroin traffic due to tighter border controls and a shortage of commercial shipping vessels. That's when dealers increased the practice of cutting their shipments with sugar, quinine or other substances. By the end of World War II, the American addict population had dropped considerably. However, several years after the war, the drug syndicates were again flourishing. The Mafia in America played a significant role in distributing heroin to urban populations. By the 1960s, Southeast Asia was involved in large-scale heroin production, providing a new source of the drug for America. During the 1960s and early 1970s, some American soldiers stationed in Southeast Asia, where heroin was plentiful, became addicts.

[51] McCoy and Read, "Heroin: The History of a 'Miracle Drug.'"

Chapter 4

The War Against Heroin

The 1960s, 1970s, and 1980s witnessed a dramatic rise in the use of recreational drugs in the United States. During these years, use of marijuana, LSD, other hallucinogens, and cocaine increased by leaps and bounds among the middle-class population. Public and government reaction to these drugs was at first ambivalent. During the 1960s and 1970s, a significant segment of the population, mostly members of the Baby Boomer generation, had begun to think that certain recreational drugs, such as marijuana and other hallucinogens, did not represent a serious danger to individual users or to society and that these drugs should be legalized. Meanwhile, a crisis in heroin use was decimating lower class urban populations, and the need to feed addictions was contributing to the crime rate. In addition, members of the armed forces stationed in Vietnam were becoming addicted to heroin. Then, in the mid-1980s, crack, a stronger, cheaper, easily prepared form of cocaine, hit the streets. Heroin, cocaine, and crack cocaine couldn't easily be defended by those liberals who had endorsed the softer recreational drugs. Rising crime rates among heroin addicts and crack addicts and strong stands against all drugs by such public figures as First Lady Nancy Reagan shifted public opinion against the use of drugs in general.

Former First Lady Nancy Reagan, who crusaded against drugs and helped to shift public opinion against the use of drugs in general.

In 1973, the U.S. Department of Justice had established the Drug Enforcement Administration (DEA), which merged the functions of four separate law enforcement agencies. With offices nationwide and in over forty foreign countries, the DEA began working to reduce the supply of domestic illegal drugs and to keep these drugs from entering the country. In 1982, the Federal Bureau of Investigation (FBI) was also given jurisdiction over illicit drug activity. The two organizations began working together on drug law enforcement and other anti-drug programs.

By 1986, the federal government had decided to take a militant stand against the use of illicit drugs in the United States. The Anti-Drug Abuse Acts, which were signed into law in 1986 and 1988, specified harsh punishment for those caught either selling or possessing illegal drugs. These anti-drug laws imposed nonnegotiable prison terms on anyone caught with a certain amount of illegal drugs, even if the person was a first-time offender or a very minor cog in a large drug ring. As a result, the prisons were filled to bursting with drug offenders. By the late 1990s, more than 60 percent of inmates in federal prisons were there for drug-related crimes.[52] However, of the approximately 20,000 federal drug offenders sentenced in 1999, only forty-one were major players in the drug-dealing business.[53]

A sense of urgency about drug abuse in the United States also led to other militant, high-cost measures by the government. Now it became commonplace for the media

[52] David G. Savage, "New Century's Bad Habits? It's a Roll of the Vice," *Los Angeles Times*, December 28, 1999.

[53] Savage, "New Century's Bad Habits? It's a Roll of the Vice."

and government officials to talk about the "war on drugs." The Anti-Drug Abuse Acts created an Office of National Drug Policy that was set up by the executive branch of the federal government. Its director became known as the "drug czar." The drug czar's job was to coordinate drug-policing efforts and the anti-drug efforts of private organizations nationwide, to help users get off drugs, and to publicize developments in the war on drugs in a way that would discourage people from becoming new users.

Under President Clinton and his drug czar, Barry McCaffrey, the government began to wage war against drugs on thirty battlegrounds, which they referred to as "High Intensity Drug Trafficking Areas."[54] These areas ranged from the Mexican border to the streets of some of the country's cities. In these areas, local, state, federal, and military agencies began working closely together to combat the distribution and use of drugs. Law enforcement agencies in some of these areas began creating computer networks of drug offenders that contained photographs of every person arrested for a drug-related crime.

The United States also stepped up efforts to control the smuggling of drugs into the country. One striking example of these efforts is a specially designed airplane, known as the Boeing E-3 Airborne Warning and Control System, which has a gigantic radar dome on top of its 707 fuselage.[55] Each of these planes costs more than $270 million to build. The planes search the air for aircraft that may be smuggling heroin or cocaine into America and then

---

[54] David Ho, Associated Press, "U.S. Drug War Detailed in Report," December 15, 1999. AOL News. My News (News Profiles).

[55] George Coryell, "Plane That Sniffs Out Drug Smugglers Nests in Tampa," *Tampa Tribune*, December 19, 1999.

warns law enforcement teams. They also alert law enforcement teams in Colombia and other countries, who are supposed to waylay the planes if they land there.[56]

According to the DEA, most of the heroin that reaches the United States today comes from Colombia and Mexico. Southwest Asia and Southeast Asia, once the primary sources for heroin on the east coast, now play relatively minor roles. The American Mafia, which once was a major player in heroin distribution, has gotten out of the heroin trade. The task of heroin distribution has become mostly the responsibility of dealers who have Caribbean, Mexican, or South American connections.

In 1998, the DEA maintained that 65 percent of the heroin seized in the United Sates came from South America. Another 17 percent came from Mexico. Practically all of the six metric tons of heroin produced in Colombia in 1998 found its way to the United States, having been smuggled there in quantities of 1 or 2 kilograms.[57]

Heroin began to reach the United States from South America in large quantities in 1993, when several independent Colombian trafficking groups, which already controlled the cocaine market, decided to expand into heroin-selling. Criminal groups from the Dominican Republic acted as retail-level distributors for the Colombians in east coast cities, providing drugs low in cost and high in purity.[58]

Almost all the heroin produced in Mexico is shipped to the United States as well; Mexican heroin tends to

---

[56] Coryell, "Plane That Sniffs Out Drug Smugglers Nests in Tampa."

[57] "Drugs of Concern: Heroin," Drug Enforcement Administration (DEA) on the Internet, home page: http://www.dea.gov/concern/heroin.htm

[58] "Drugs of Concern: Heroin."

dominate the west coast. Couriers have been bringing the heroin across the border in larger and larger amounts. One shipment captured by the DEA weighed 55 pounds.[59] Mexican heroin is distributed in the United States by Mexican-American gangs and other criminal organizations.

As already stated, heroin from Southwest and Southeast Asia has begun to play a less significant role in this country. Southwest Asian heroin comes from, Iran, Pakistan, Turkey, and especially Afghanistan. Trafficking is done by tightly knit family and ethnic groups from these regions, who work in New York City, Baltimore, Washington, DC, Los Angeles, San Diego, San Francisco, and a few midwestern cities.[60] Southeast Asian heroin, which comes from the "Golden Triangle" region of Burma, Thailand, and Laos, is still arriving in America, but its volume has been severely reduced by the South American competition. Finally, criminal organizations in Nigeria and West Africa, with connections in Southeast and Southwest Asia, are also involved in heroin distribution in this country. Some work in the Chicago area, where they have developed a large dealing network.[61]

It has become clear to the U.S. government that heroin smuggling into this country cannot be stopped without international cooperation. Accordingly, in the year 2000, Colombia prepared to launch a major U.S.-backed offensive against its burgeoning drug trade. Congress approved a record $1.3 billion for this purpose, which was targeted

---

[59] "Drugs of Concern: Heroin."

[60] "Drugs of Concern: Heroin."

[61] "Drugs of Concern: Heroin."

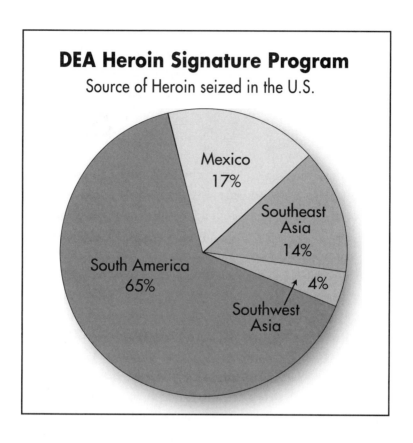

DEA Heroin Signature Program
Source of Heroin seized in the U.S.

Mexico
17%

Southeast
Asia
14%

4%

Southwest
Asia

South America
65%

mostly for military anti-drug maneuvers.[62] The offensive seems to be proving to be effective. During 2000, for example, the Colombian government's seizures of heroin and cocaine destined for export more than doubled. Near the end of that same year, Colombian police and the DEA arrested forty-nine people who were part of a major international heroin and cocaine smuggling network. Based in

---

[62] Reuters Limited, "Colombian Says U.S. Covered Up Heroin Scam," July 12, 2000. Archived by MAP: The Media Awareness Project, a feature of DrugSense, on the Internet at: http://www.mapinc.org/

the city of Medellín, this cartel was part of a new generation of low-profile traffickers who had come up after Pablo Escobar, the leader of a flashier Medellín cartel, was tracked down and killed in 1993. This new low-profile cartel had shipped approximately 13.5 tons of cocaine and heroin to the United States before authorities caught them.[63]

The U.S.-backed Colombian anti-drug effort is ambiguously intertwined with the Colombian government's campaign against Marxist rebels, whom Colombian officials have accused of trafficking in narcotics. This places the U.S. involvement in Colombian anti-drug activities in a context that is concerned with the internal politics of Colombia, and not just with drug smuggling.

In addition, anti-drug operations in Colombia have already been plagued by resignations and scandals. After less than a year, General Ismael Trujillo Polanco, director of the counter-narcotics division of the National Police and a key player in the government's anti-drug efforts, opted for early retirement and was replaced.[64] A few months earlier, a former chauffeur at the U.S. embassy in Bogotá accused U.S. officials of covering up some of the details of a sensational heroin-smuggling ring that involved a U.S. military commander and his wife.

According to the chauffeur, Jorge Ayala, DEA officials helped smuggle heroin from Colombia to the United States while U.S. Marine guards looked the other way.[65] The chauffeur was alluding to a military scandal that was

---

[63] Jared Kotler, Associated Press, "49 Arrested in Colombia Drug Ring," November 1, 2000. AOL News. My News (News Profiles).

[64] Reuters Limited, "Colombian Anti-drugs Chief Steps Down," October 25, 2000. AOL News. My News (News Profiles).

[65] Reuters Limited, "Colombian Says U.S. Covered Up Heroin Scam."

brought to light in the United States early in 2000. Colonel James C. Hiett was a key administrator of U.S. anti-drug operations in Colombia, overseeing approximately two hundred American troops whose job it was to train Colombian security forces in counter-narcotics operations. All the while his wife was shipping heroin from the United States Embassy in Bogotá to contacts in Manhattan and Queens. In January 2000 Laurie Anne Hiett pleaded guilty to drug trafficking and was sentenced to prison for five years.[66] About 13 pounds of heroin worth $700,000 were shipped, and the profits from the shipments were laundered.[67] The colonel admitted to paying bills with profits from his wife's drug sales. For not reporting her activities, he was sentenced to five months in prison.[68]

Meanwhile, throughout the world, the governments of other heroin-producing nations are asking for help on an international scale. For example, near the end of 2000, the government of Myanmar, a Southeast Asian country that is the world's second largest producer of opium and heroin[69] after Afghanistan, put out an SOS begging cooperation from its Asian neighbors in its fight against drug producers and traffickers. The country has limited resources for fighting drug-smuggling activities along its 3,600 miles of borders with Thailand, Laos, China, and India.

[66] Alan Feuer, "Army Colonel Sentenced for Not Reporting Wife's Heroin Smuggling," *New York Times*, July 14, 2000.

[67] Reuters Limited, "Colombian Says U.S. Covered Up Heroin Scam."

[68] Feuer, "Army Colonel Sentenced for Not Reporting Wife's Heroin Smuggling."

[69] Nopporn Wong-Anan, "Myanmar Says Can't Fight Drug Trade Alone," Reuters Limited, October 11, 2000. AOL News. My News (News Profiles).

Around the same time that Myanmar was asking for help, the Taliban government of Afghanistan ordered a total ban on poppy cultivation, threatening severe punishments for any farmers who continued to grow it.[70] This order went hand in hand with tightened United Nations surveillance of Afghanistan's Tajik border. This surveillance may have been partly responsible for a dramatic drop in opium production revenues during 2000. Revenues for poppy production in 2000 fell to about $90 million, compared to the $230 million average for opium production in previous years.[71] However, no one knows how much of the drop was caused by increased surveillance and how much was due to a severe drought that same year which reduced opium poppy crop yields. Whatever the reason for decline, it is certain to have a dramatic effect on the international heroin supply. Afghanistan supplies as much as 75 percent of the world's opium, reaching Europe through the ex-Soviet states of Central Asia.[72]

Opinions concerning the efficacy of the U.S. war on drugs differ widely. Prison inmate activists and drug rehabilitation lobbyists living in the United States have sharply criticized the government for its draconian anti-drug laws. These activists believe that the money needed to house a first-time drug offender in prison can be better spent on an increase in rehabilitation programs. Others have criticized

---

[70] Reuters Limited, "Afghan Taliban Orders Poppy Cultivation Ban," October 29, 2000. AOL News. My News (News Profiles).

[71] Reuters Limited, "Afghan Drug Production Fell Sharply in 2000—UN," October 20, 2000. AOL News. My News (News Profiles).

[72] Reuters Limited, "Afghan Drug Production Fell Sharply in 2000—UN."

the war on drugs for its entanglements with politics, charging that through its international strategies against the drug trade our country sometimes supports oppressive governments. Some think that the ultimate cure for the drug abuse problem in America is the decriminalization of all drugs, which would immediately end illicit dealing in them and create a more wholesome environment for drug use.

In October 2000, however, Pino Arlacchi, who heads the international fight against illegal drugs, announced that he thought the current war on drugs was being won. Arlacchi is executive director of the United Nations Office for Drug Control and Crime Prevention. His goal is to fulfill a 1998 UN pledge to completely eliminate world cultivation of the opium poppy and coca bush by the year 2008. Arlacchi's strategy is to convince farmers to cultivate legal crops instead of opium or coca, both by offering them incentives and by using some coercion. According to Arlacchi, this approach is working. The area of land devoted to the cultivation of illegal crops has decreased by 15 percent in recent years. Nevertheless, critics feel that the United Nations Office for Drug Control and Crime Prevention faces a nearly hopeless struggle. The agency has an annual budget of about $70 million whereas the international drug trade brings in about $400 billion annually.[73]

In October 2000, in an effort to strangle Mexican heroin exportation at its root, the DEA added twelve Mexicans to its most wanted list. Two of them had been associates of a deceased drug trafficker named Amado Carrillo, who ran a powerful Juarez cartel that dealt heroin, cocaine,

---

[73] Timofei Zhukov, Associated Press, "Asian Countries Join Drug War," October 20, 2000. AOL News. My News (News Profiles).

and marijuana. There are other high-level drug cartels in Mexico as well, such as the Arellano-Felix Brothers gang in Tijuana and the Caro-Quintero cartel in Sonora.[74]

Traffickers from Mexico and Colombia often employ down-and-out couriers to smuggle heroin and other drugs across the border. These couriers, known as "mules," are at first attracted by the fees they are offered, which tend to range from $4,000 to $6,000 a trip—more than they may make from legitimate work in an entire year. Often they do not find out how they are to transport the drugs until they have agreed to take the job and have met with higher-level smugglers. Then they may be ordered to swallow balloons or condoms containing the drug. Once over the border, they are supposed to pass the packaged drugs from their body through the use of prune juice and laxatives. However, sometimes the balloons or condoms burst before they are excreted. Then those who swallowed them may end up in a hospital or dead.[75]

In June 2000, federal authorities arrested thirty-two members of a huge Mexican-based heroin organization that maintained a major distribution center in San Diego. Investigators had been working for two years to dismantle the organization through a campaign they dubbed Operation Black Tar. These arrests brought the total to 280. The organization was shipping 80 to 100 pounds of black tar heroin a month to the United States from Tijuana and other points along the southwestern border. Ringleaders based in Los Angeles directed the distribution nationwide.

---

74 Pav Jodan, Reuters Limited, "DEA Puts 12 Mexicans on 'Most Wanted' List," October 16, 2000. AOL News. My News (News Profiles).

75 Chris Gaither, "Courier's Stomach Yields Heroin Load," *Miami Herald*, July 19, 2000.

These dealers in black tar heroin had a particularly repulsive strategy for finding customers. They would focus on local methadone clinics in the Southwest, offering patients free samples of the drug. They even recruited employees at the clinics to lure addicts to shooting galleries that had been set up. Shipments from the organization are thought to have caused the deaths of eighty-five people in Chimayo, New Mexico.[76]

Successful stings by the DEA and other drug-enforcement agencies have earned them a lot of publicity. Unfortunately, certain oversights have worked to tarnish their image as well. In September 2000 the media charged that federal monitoring of the use of street drugs by university researchers was overly lax. The government provides about $250 million each year to university research teams studying the effects of heroin, cocaine and other drugs. Several thousand researchers are registered by the DEA to conduct experiments with these drugs. Only about five are authorized to use the hardest drugs, which include heroin. The drugs come from police raids or from legitimate laboratories. In general, once the researchers have passed background checks and have had their research approved, the DEA is unlikely to monitor them closely. There have been several publicized incidents in which researchers have taken the drugs for recreational purposes and have overdosed. On several occasions, too, drugs being used for research were stolen from laboratories.[77]

Is there a just and effective way to regulate the use of mind-altering substances in America? Can law enforcement

---

[76] Marisa Taylor and Joe Cantlupe, "Huge Heroin Ring Broken by U.S. as 280 Arrested," *San Diego Union Tribune*, June 16, 2000.

[77] Karen Gullo, Associated Press, "Federal Monitoring of Researchers' Use of Street Drugs Lax," *Houston Chronicle*, December 30, 1999.

officials ever win the daunting international war against drugs? To date, no one has been able to answer these questions. America's increasingly dissonant relationship to opiates has raised fears in every segment of society. And none of the proposed solutions seems sufficient.

One solution, however, has distinct advantages. It involves approaching the drug problem from the standpoint of the individual. We may not be able to win total control over international drug cartels or the criminal distribution of addictive substances, but we may be able to vanquish addiction one person at a time through the processes of treatment and recovery.

Chapter 5

Roads to Recovery

Jazz insiders remember Jimmie Maxwell,[78] a talented trumpet player who toured with Benny Goodman, Lionel Hampton, and Duke Ellington. Now over eighty years of age, he lives with his wife in Great Neck, New York. During a tour with Benny Goodman in the Soviet Union in the 1960s, Jimmie fell ill with a chronic case of diarrhea. Soviet doctors treated it with laudanum, a mixture of alcohol and opium. The experience gave Maxwell a taste for the opiate high. When he got back to the states, he began to experiment with heroin and became an addict. His addiction had such a hold over him that he considered suicide. These days Maxwell dissolves a rather large

---

[78] Christopher S. Wren, "One of Medicine's Best-kept Secrets: Methadone Works," *New York Times* Archives, June 3, 1997.

orange-colored tablet in water each morning and drinks the solution down. The tablet is methadone, a drug Maxwell has relied on for the last thirty-two years.

Jimmie Maxwell represents the high-end of the spectrum of addiction treatment successes. Methadone, which is a synthetic opiate, has kept him away from heroin for more than three decades. Methadone itself is addictive, but drug treatment professionals think it has several advantages over heroin. It can be taken orally instead of being injected. It prevents withdrawal symptoms in people taking heroin; one dose a day is enough. It does not produce a debilitating high once a person becomes used to it, and it has few proven long-term harmful effects. Methadone for heroin addicts has been compared to insulin for diabetics. It is a long-term therapy for a chronic condition.

About 115,000 American rehabilitated heroin addicts rely on methadone as a way of avoiding heroin. But not all of them adapt to it as well as Jimmie Maxwell has. In fact, only about 5 to 20 percent stay on it for more than ten years.[79] The rest relapse into heroin use or manage to get off all medication and avoid heroin as well. Methadone itself does have an abuse potential. Although it is usually distributed daily in a licensed clinic, people who take it in daily doses must take two doses home for the weekend when the clinic will be closed. Some of this methadone that leaves the clinic finds its way to the streets, where it is sold as a get-high drug. Also, some people on methadone maintenance continue to abuse other drugs, such as tranquilizers, opiates, and cocaine, which interact with the methadone dose to produce a powerful high.

To date, no one has discovered a foolproof cure for

---

[79] Wren, "One of Medicine's Best-Kept Secrets: Methadone Works."

Methadone tablets.

heroin addiction. Treatments range from the substitution of other more manageable drugs, such as methadone, to complete detoxification from heroin, followed by counseling and rehabilitation. One thing, however, is clear. Treatment for drug addiction, when it works, is a much more cost-effective way of dealing with the heroin problem than incarceration. It costs upwards of $20,000 to keep one person in prison for a year; it costs approximately $4,000 to offer that same person a year of treatment and counseling for addiction.[80] As recently estimated, for every $1 spent on drug addiction treatment, there is a $4 to $7 reduction in drug-related crime.[81] Other less easily measurable benefits include increased productivity in the workplace and fewer drug-related accidents at work, at home, and on the road.

In October 2000, California introduced a ballot measure that would require treatment instead of prison for nonviolent first- and second-time minor drug offenders. Some high-level politicians, like San Francisco mayor Willie Brown, supported the initiative. Others, like actor Martin Sheen, whose son nearly died of a drug overdose in 1998, spoke out against it. Sheen and others believe that only the fear of punishment can keep some people off drugs. They see punitive measures as one aspect of treatment for addiction. However, if the bill is passed, 36,000 offenders a year will be given the option of treatment over prison.[82] At the time this book is being written, the vote had not yet taken place.

---

[80] Don Thompson, Associated Press, "California Bill Would Treat Drug Users," October 24, 2000. AOL News. My News (News Profiles).

[81] In *Principles of Drug Addiction Treatment: A Research–based Guide*, National Institute on Drug Abuse, 2000.

[82] Thompson, "California Bill Would Treat Drug Users."

In 1998, a government survey indicated that treatment can be highly beneficial to addicts and their communities. The survey found that addicts who underwent treatment were much less likely to use illegal drugs or commit drug-related crimes for as long as five years after the treatment terminated. Those who were treated with methadone seemed to show the most dramatic improvement. The only exception seemed to be adolescents, whose abuse of drugs was not significantly lowered by treatment strategies.[83]

As mentioned in chapter 3, addiction was not classified as an illness in the first decades of the twentieth century. Then, in 1914, the Harrison Act prevented doctors from treating addicts with any kind of opiate. Supplying an addict with such drugs, even if it were for the purpose of weaning him off heroin, was considered to be collaborating in his addiction.

Today, the general attitude is that addiction, like cancer or heart disease, is a life-threatening disease that deserves treatment by the use of medication, by behavioral therapies, or by a combination of the two. Studies of the physiological, psychological, and social elements of addiction have led to new advances in the treatment of addicts. In July 2000, the House of Representatives voted 412–1 to approve legislation known as the Drug Addiction Treatment Act.[84] The new law would allow qualified private physicians to treat opiate-dependent patients with synthetic opiates and other drugs. This would make it easier for addicts to get

---

[83] Christopher S. Wren, "Study Finds Treatment Aids Addicts." *New York Times* Archives, September 12, 1998.

[84] Reuters Limited, "House Approves Heroin Treatment Bill," July 20, 2000. Archived by MAP: The Media Awareness Project, a feature of DrugSense, on the internet at: http://www.mapinc.org/

treatment in areas that do not have government-approved addiction treatment clinics. It might also protect the anonymity of some addicts by making the problem something that only their doctors have to know about.

Following is a description of some of the single and combination drug therapies that have helped people wanting to get off heroin, including a new drug therapy that is on the verge of being approved in this country.

Methadone. Methadone was invented in 1943 in Germany to replace morphine, which had become scarce during World War II. It was first conceived of as a painkiller, but it never achieved widespread use until the 1960s, when American researchers Vincent Dole and Marie Nyswander developed a program that used it to treat heroin addiction.

In addicts, one dose of methadone prevents withdrawal symptoms and drug craving for 24 hours. It also blocks the euphoric effects of an average dose of heroin if they use that drug simultaneously. Patients on methadone receive between 20 to 120 milligrams once a day. The amount of the dose depends partly on how much heroin they consumed regularly before they began treatment. Eventually, a patient may choose to be weaned off methadone, and the dose is lowered gradually.

Methadone has been proven to work best when it is combined with other treatment strategies. These include psychotherapy and group recovery programs, such as Narcotics Anonymous. Regular urinalysis, in which a patient's urine is studied for signs of recent illicit drug use, has also made treatment with methadone more effective. Several research studies have shown that methadone combined with a reward system for addicts who stay clean, such as gifts or prizes, and a punitive system, which penalizes those addicts who fail urinalysis tests, produced the best results.[85]

LAAM.   Levo-alpha-acetylmethadol (LAAM) is a synthetic opiate that resembles methadone. Its advantage over methadone is that it can block opiate withdrawal symptoms for up to 72 hours. Like methadone, it can be taken orally, and it has few known harmful side effects. The Food and Drug Administration approved the use of LAAM to treat heroin addiction in 1993. It has to be taken only three times a week, which eliminates the problem of weekend doses. Methadone is still the drug of choice in the treatment of heroin addiction, but LAAM is becoming increasingly popular. However, LAAM is more expensive than methadone. A week of LAAM maintenance costs about $51 versus about $39 a week for methadone maintenance.[86]

Naloxone and Naltrexone.   These drugs are opiate antagonists. They block or reverse the effects of heroin, morphine and the other opiates. This means that if a person who has taken naloxone or naltrexone consumes an opiate, no pleasurable effects from the opiate will be felt. These substances can also be used as antidotes to acute opiate intoxication. However, if they are administered to an addict while on a high, they will immediately cause painful withdrawal symptoms. They are useful in saving lives by reversing opiate intoxication in acute cases of overdose. They are

---

[85] "NIDA Research Priorities and Highlights." Drug Abuse and Addiction Research, Sixth Triennial Report to Congress, 1999, National Institute on Drug Abuse, National Institutes of Health, U.S. Department of Health and Human Services.

[86] Susan Gill Vardon, "Medical Options Growing: Alternatives to Methadone Endorsed by Some," *Fort-Worth Star-Telegram*, April 27, 1998.

also used by highly motivated recovered addicts who are willing to put themselves in a long-term situation where it is not possible to experience the pleasurable effects of heroin. Naltrexone is the longer-acting of the two and will block the pleasurable effects of opiates for one to three days.

Buprenorphine. Buprenorphine is another opiate that, like methadone, helps curb heroin withdrawal. It has been used in injectable form as a pain-killer in hospitals for many years, but its use as a treatment for heroin addiction is relatively recent. In the last few years, it has been administered quite successfully in France to treat large numbers of heroin addicts. Large-scale studies there showed that its use could improve the mental health, physical health, and socioeconomic functioning of a significant number of patients. Buprenorphine produces a high, but a much milder one than heroin. Patients on this opiate can function at work or drive cars.

Buprenorphine is also thought to be easier to withdraw from than heroin or methadone. When it is combined with naloxone, one of the opiate antagonists, it is less likely to be abused, and addicts won't resort to other opiates either. Buprenorphine is long-lasting; a dose lasts about 72 hours. It has not yet received FDA approval, but researchers and a few doctors have been using it to treat heroin addicts in the United States. At the Kolmac Clinic in Silver Springs, Maryland, it is being used as an "off-label" treatment for heroin addicts.[87] "Off-label" means that the drug is on the market but has not yet been designated for the purpose for which it is being used. One concern about buprenorphine

---

[87] Fredrick Kunkle, "A Not-Quite-Legal-Lifeline; Approval Nears on Promising Treatment for Narcotics Addiction," *Washington Post*, August 21, 2000.

that remains unresolved is whether or not it can damage the liver. Slight toxicity to the liver has been recorded but only in a very small minority of cases.

NOS Inhibitors. NOS inhibitors are chemicals that inhibit the enzyme nitric oxide synthase. Some inhibitors have been found to reduce the symptoms of opiate withdrawal. NOS inhibitors might be useful for those patients who decide to detoxify from heroin, helping them through the worst stages of the withdrawal process.

DETOX AND RECOVERY

An option that is always open to the addict is full detoxification from heroin without the additional use of a maintenance drug. Addicts have tried various methods by themselves to kick their habit, but none can eliminate the three or four days of severe withdrawal symptoms. In a medical setting, aids for this process are available. Tranquilizers, anti-convulsants, and other drugs like the NOS inhibitors can alleviate some of the symptoms of "kicking." However, the process is never stress-free. Generally, detoxification from heroin entails a three- to seven-day in-hospital treatment. Jody, a twenty-nine-year-old addict, who has gone through the detox process three times, described it as follows:

> *Kicking isn't as bad as people say. At least, for me it wasn't. It really depends on how deep you are into your addiction. How much heroin you been taking before you go into detox. The lighter your addiction, the easier it is to kick…*
>
> *I've never done it on my own, only in clinics. It's pretty much like this: you go in and they assign you a bed.*

The first day seems like the worst. Sweating and you can feel your heart beating in your chest and your calves kinking up in spasms... What I remember getting at the clinic to help with my withdrawal was clonidine, which keeps your blood pressure from skyrocketing. And pheno- barbital, which calms down your muscles and cuts the goose bumps... It isn't that bad, but if I wasn't doing it in the clinic, I couldn't have gone through it...

I've kicked from heroin, straight from the needle to the clinic. And from methadone, after lowering the methadone dose over a period of months. It was easier to get off the low-dose methadone, but not that easy...

One thing that I do when I feel I'm jumping out of my skin, if I can, is push-ups. I work myself up until I can feel the blood in my skin. It makes it easier.

In recent years, another, more radical treatment known as ultra-rapid opiate detoxification (UROD) has been offered to some addicts. It is a five- to six-hour procedure available at some hospitals or clinics in New York, Chicago and California. During this process, the patient is rendered unconscious with anesthesia and then administered an opiate antagonist such as naltrexone. Withdrawal, precipitated by the antagonist, is lightning-quick and quite violent. But since the patient is unconscious, he or she is not thought to experience the symptoms. However, the anesthesia itself can be life threatening, and this method has resulted in a few deaths. Many professionals think it is too risky. At this time, it remains a marginal treatment that is not recommended by most addiction-treatment authorities.

After three or four days, the acute symptoms of heroin withdrawal disappear, but other symptoms may stay with the user for weeks or even months. These may include sleeplessness or nightmares, nervousness, depression and cravings for heroin. Long-term heroin use is a radical numbing of the nervous system. Now, as physiological and emotional processes that have been suppressed return, a person may experience all kinds of distressing symptoms. Problems that have been avoided are suddenly staring you in the face. The French writer and filmmaker Jean Cocteau, who was a long-term opium addict, likened opiate intoxication to the season of winter, in which natural processes are temporarily frozen, put in hibernation. He said that withdrawal and detoxification had the violence of spring coming. It was like sap suddenly rising in a plant.

To date, scientists still don't understand all the changes that take place in the brain during heroin intoxication, withdrawal or recovery. They are beginning to understand how the dopamine receptors work in the brain during these processes, but they suspect that other factors are at work. A new emphasis in addiction research has shifted from the dopamine pleasure centers of the brain to other mechanisms. Scientists have become particularly interested in "emotional memories"—mental records of events that trigger powerful emotions. These reactions are thought to be formed in the amygdala, a small structure deep inside the brain.[88] One of the hardest things for recovered addicts to deal with are enticing memories of the high. These can be triggered by the sight of drug paraphernalia or a visit to a location or person that one associates with getting high. It is thought that emotional memories re-trigger the addiction in reaction to these stimuli, putting the recovered addict in

---

[88] "Denise Grady, "Hardest Habit to Break: Memories of the High," *New York Times*, October 26, 1998.

danger of starting again. That is one reason why recovery programs stress avoidance of old crowds and old locations associated with one's past drug use.

Worthwhile detox programs include some kind of follow-up therapy after the initial three to seven days. This may include individual psychotherapy, group therapy, recovery-group participation, or medications such as anti-depressants or opiate antagonists. The recovery processes offered by self-help groups like Narcotics Anonymous have helped thousands of addicts get through the difficult first few months and stay drug free. Solidarity with other addicts and self-discovery are two mainstays of these processes. Many recovered addicts swear by them.

Residential drug treatment programs, like Phoenix House, with facilities throughout the country, make use of the recovery process that developed in the self-help net-work. Phoenix House stresses group solidarity, community membership with strong rules and sanctions, and a radical deconstruction of egotistical illusions. Those who come to Phoenix House and other residential drug treatment pro-grams learn to come to terms with the lies they have been hiding behind. They learn, hopefully, to get to the bottom of the low self-esteem that led to their addiction. And they learn to take responsibility for their actions and to accept the consequences of slacking off. For some, the benefits are striking. For the first time in their lives, they feel that they are facing their feelings. They learn to take each day one at a time and to accept their lives as they are. Once this process has taken hold, recovered addicts usually need help adapting to society at large. Education programs, job training, and assisted living arrangements can help them get back on their feet.

There are no guarantees that residential drug programs

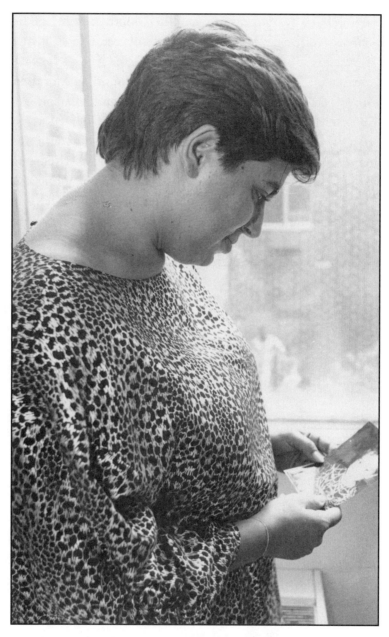

A patient at the Phoenix House drug rehabilitation center in New York City looks at a photograph of her son.

will work for everyone, but when they do, the results can be impressive. Tone, a thirty-year-old recovered addict, is one of Phoenix House's success stories. He is from Newark, New Jersey and is of Puerto Rican background. His mother, who speaks no English, was a drug abuser and an alcoholic. To escape continual violence perpetrated by her addicted boyfriends against his mother and against him and his younger brother, Tone left home at fifteen. At sixteen he was an addict and dealer who spent most days hanging out at Port Authority, New York City's main bus terminal. He slept where he could, sometimes in the terminal lavatories, and sometimes he traded sexual favors for a bed. He became a member of the Latin Kings and a father by the age of seventeen.

Tone got through life by convincing himself that he had the skills of an adult. "I can handle it," accompanied by a macho swagger, was his way of facing the riskiest or most sordid situations. Heroin helped him maintain a hyper-macho image of himself. It was like living in a total fantasy world. When he was high, he wasn't a homeless teenager with a drug problem in flight from an abusive home. He was a leader of the pack and the lord of Port Authority.

At seventeen, an overdose landed him in the hospital. He detoxed and, since it was winter, rather than go back to the street, he accepted the suggestion that he check into Phoenix House. He didn't know what he was agreeing to. At first, the Phoenix House residential program seemed like boot camp to him. Each small infraction that he committed—not making his bed, appearing late for meals—had a consequence. He spent an entire week wearing a sign that said, "I think I'm too good to clean my room." Most of each day was spent in encounter groups. Other recovering addicts began to pick apart his image. At first, he felt as if he were being senselessly taunted. You think you're a big man, they told him, but you're really an infant who hates himself, who's crying because he lost his mama. Meanwhile, there were professionals poised to help when he needed individual counseling or was sick with a cold or other minor illnesses. For the first time in his life, people were taking care of him. He ate well, slept in a clean, warm bed, and was surrounded by people with whom he began to identify—fellow addicts who'd been through what he went through. As the days passed, his increasing distance from heroin use began to feel like an accomplishment. He realized that for the first time he was truly proud of what he was able to do. The encounter groups changed him as well. He dropped his macho pose and became more honest, more humble. He was also astonished by the feelings of warmth that poured out of him for those around him. New arrivals especially aroused his emotions. He felt he understood their feelings and wanted to help them.

Tone stayed at Phoenix House for almost three years. He was younger than most of the residents and he had nowhere else to go, so the staff decided to keep him long enough for him to develop an identity and gain some education. He graduated from high school while at Phoenix House and was the salutatorian of his class. Today, he works as a nurse's aide and is married to a woman who works at the same hospital. He's been drug free for over eleven years.

UNUSUAL SOLUTIONS

Two unusual approaches to the problem of heroin addiction will close this chapter. These approaches aren't treatments but methods of harm reduction. Harm reduction is a public health strategy that seeks to limit the harm done by dangerous practices like shooting heroin without trying to stop the practices themselves.

This first method of harm reduction isn't practiced in the United States, but has gained great headway in Switzerland. It involves doling out heroin to addicts in a controlled setting in state-sanctioned clinics. In 1999, Swiss voters endorsed this method of treatment because they believed it led to harm reduction for long-term addicts. Heroin users are given access to rooms with sterile syringes, cotton, spoons, bandages, rubber tourniquets, and heroin. Medical practitioners are available to instruct them in proper injection techniques or to help if a bad reaction or overdose occurs. The existence of safe injection rooms has caused quite a bit of fallout in Switzerland and in the world at large. Some medical professionals in both Switzerland and the United States and members of the World Health Organization have sharply criticized this program. They claim that it encourages people to use heroin and that the research behind the program was not based on controlled studies. At the present time, however, the program has the full support of the government.

In San Francisco, a program known as UFO, or You Find Out, seeks to save the lives of young intravenous heroin users. The team that runs UFO became interested in preventing drug overdoses after researching the AIDS epidemic and hepatitis B and C for fifteen years. Addicts who use needles are vulnerable to all three of these diseases. The UFO team began to talk to the addicts they encountered about overdoses, which they define as a state of cyanosis, in which the extremities are not getting enough oxygen. If the lips or fingers of a user have turned blue, then the user has experienced an overdose as it is defined by UFO.

The UFO team discovered that about three quarters of

the addicts they treat had had such an experience or witnessed it, but only about a tenth had died from it. UFO now runs regular training sessions on how to save the life of a person who has overdosed. Addicts are taught to call 911 and to perform CPR to get the person breathing again. Finding a way to get the overdose victim breathing again is essential because heroin kills by depressing the respiratory reflex.

UFO is also doing a survey of street drug use and street treatment. They screen for HIV and hepatitis during this process. Being part of the street study raises users' consciousness about the hazards of heroin use without subjecting them to judgmental lectures or sanctions. UFO also provides users with medical referrals for heroin-related problems.

Of course, few believe that any treatment program can totally solve the heroin crisis in American society. Even those groups that feel heroin should be decriminalized or doled out according to the Swiss model do not claim that they have discovered the philosopher's stone that lies at the very root of the addiction puzzle. There are no easy solutions. The extreme penalizations for drug use instituted by the anti-drug abuse laws of the 1980s have jammed our prisons with new inmates but haven't come close to ending the drug abuse problem. Treatment programs have generated some proven degree of success, but all of them require individual motivation and commitment. What about the heroin user who isn't inspired by such impulses?

Heroin abuse is perplexing because of the many questions it raises. How is addiction related to poverty and early negative childhood experiences? Is the addicted personality a result of genetics? How much responsibility should the individual drug user take for his or her problem? How much should be laid in the lap of society? When do opiates stop being medicine and begin to become harmful substances? How much power should the medical profession be given to deal with the problem of heroin addiction? Why is heroin addiction increasingly becoming a middle-class problem? Is the problem a psychotherapeutic or a moral one?

Perhaps some of these questions will be answered as researchers make further inroads into the physiological and psychological causes of addiction. But regardless of theories, laws, judgments or daring new approaches to the question of drugs, heroin continues to form a very personal bond with its users. Heroin addiction is a story of real people and a very demanding drug, a controlling drug. Once heroin has settled in, an addict's story becomes remarkably like that of all the other addicts. Without rehabilitation, that story becomes, in most cases, the story of pleasure turned sour, the story of an adventure that led to a dead-end existence of desperation and loss. The good news is that the path back is paved with new resources and new aids. And there are plenty of people taking that path together, in self-help groups and clinics. Working hand in hand, they are facing themselves and their addiction in a way that no one else can. The good news is that some of them may make it—all the way back to a drug-free life.

To Find Out More

ORGANIZATIONS AND ONLINE SITES

Addiction Resource Guide
P.O. Box 8612
Tarrytown, NY 10591
Tel. (914) 725-5151
http://www.addictionresourceguide.com/
A comprehensive online directory of addiction treatment facilities.

Addiction Solutions
http://www.addictionsolutions.com/index.asp
Treatment and Resource Locator that allows you to search locally or nationally for therapists, counseling services, interventionists, holistic practitioners, treatment centers, physicians, transitional living environments, methadone clinics, attorneys, diversion programs, hotlines, shelters, missions, and meal programs.

The Alliance Project
1954 University Avenue West, Suite 12
St. Paul, MN 55104
Tel. (651) 645-1618
Fax (651) 645-1576
http://www.defeataddiction.org/
A broad cross-section of organizations that share common concerns about the devastating disease of alcohol and drug addiction and the dramatic lack of proper public response to this growing health crisis.

Community Anti-Drug Coalitions of America
901 N. Pitt Street, Suite 300
Alexandria, VA 22314
Tel. (703) 706-0560
http://www.cadca.org/
The premier membership organization of over 5,000 community coalitions nationwide, each fighting the problems associated with substance abuse and violence— one community at a time.

Drug Enforcement Administration (DEA)
Information Services Section (CPI)
700 Army Navy Drive
Arlington, VA 22202
http://www.dea.gov
Supports, directs, and coordinates national and international programs against the distribution and abuse of illegal drugs.

Freevibe
http://www.freevibe.com
Informs teens on real effects of drugs and how to get help.

Brought to you by the National Youth Anti-Drug Media Campaign and Sony Pictures Digital Entertainment.

Hazelden Foundation
Tel. (800) 257-7810 or (615) 213-4000
http://www.hazelden.org
A nonprofit organization providing high-quality, affordable rehabilitation, education, prevention and professional services and publications in chemical dependency and related disorders.

The Lindesmith Center
925 Ninth Avenue
New York, NY, 10019
Tel. (212) 548-0695
Fax (212) 548-4670
http://www.lindesmith.org/
The leading independent drug policy institute in the United States.

Media Awareness Project
Drugnews Index
http://www.mapinc.org/
46,896 drug-related news clippings.

Narcotics Anonymous
World Service Office
P.O. Box 9999
Van Nuys, CA 91409
Tel. (818) 773-9999
http://www.wsoinc.com/
An international, community-based association of recovering drug addicts. Referrals to local programs available.

The National Alliance of Methadone Advocates
http://www.methadone.org/
Organization composed of methadone maintenance
patients and supporters of quality methadone maintenance
treatment.

**National Clearinghouse for Alcohol and Drug
Information (NCADI)**
Tel. (800) 729-6686.
Provides free publications on drug abuse, access to
counselors, and treatment referral options in your area,
nationwide.

National Institute on Drug Abuse
6001 Executive Blvd.
Bethesda, MD 20892-9561
Tel. (301) 443-1124
Supports over 85 percent of the world's research on the
health aspects of drug abuse and addiction.

Partnership for a Drug-Free America
405 Lexington Avenue, Suite 1601
New York, NY 10174
Tel. (212) 922-1560
General Inquiries: info@drugfree.org
http://www.drugfreeamerica.org/
A private nonprofit, nonpartisan coalition of professionals
from the communications industry aiming to reduce
demand for illicit drugs in America through media
communication.

Partnership for Responsible Drug Information
14 West 68th Street
New York, NY 10023
Tel. (212) 362-1964
http://www.prdi.org/
Information and discussion about the drug crisis. Guide to U.S. drug policy.

Phoenix House
New York: Tel. (800) HELP-111 (adults); (212) 873-1800, ext. 7510 (adolescents)
California: Tel. (818) 896-1121, ext. 4053 (adults & adolescents)
Florida: Tel. (352) 867-7000 (adults 18 and over only)
Texas: Tel. (512) 440-0613 (adolescents)
http://www.phoenixhouse.org/
One of the nation's leading nonprofit substance abuse service organizations, providing treatment for more than 5,000 adults and adolescents.

Prevline—Prevention Online
http://www.health.org/
World's largest resource for current information and materials concerning alcohol and substance abuse prevention, intervention, and treatment.

READINGS AND VIDEOTAPES

Heroin
by Julian Durlacher (Editor)
Carlton Books, 2000
Part of a series that tells the story of drug misuse, tracing
the history of drugs and explaining their transition to
illegal and "recreational" use.

Heroin
by Humberto Fernandez
Hazelden Information Education, 1988
Examination of the origin, use, effect, and politics
of heroin.

**Heroin: The Street Narcotic (Encyclopedia of
Psychoactive Drugs. Series 1)**
by Fred Zackon, Solomon H. Snyder (Editor), and
William E. McAulyfe
Chelsea House Publications, 1992
Examines the history, characteristics, dangers, and
rehabilitation treatment associated with heroin.

How to Stop Time: Heroin from A to Z
by Ann Marlowe
Basic Books, 1999
The story of the heroin addiction of an upper-middle-class
professional, told from a literary point of view.

Lady Sings the Blues
by Billie Holiday with William Duffy (with a revised discography)
Penguin Books, 1992 (originally published 1956)
Life story of the famous jazz singer and heroin addict.

Permanent Midnight
Videocassette. Directed by David Veloz
Film based on the memoir by Jerry Stahl, a television writer who became a heroin addict.

***The Politics of Heroin:* CIA Complicity in the Global Drug Trade**
by Alfred W. McCoy
Lawrence Hill & Co., 1991
A revised and expanded edition of McCoy's *Politics of Heroin in Southeast Asia*. Argues that in their efforts to expand their own power in Southeast Asia, American intelligence agents permitted allies of the U.S. to expand their lucrative drug trade.

Smack
by Melvin Burgess
(a young adult book)
Avon, 1999
By a winner of the Carnegie Medal and the Guardian Prize for Fiction, an artful sketch of a gradual descent into drug addiction.

Traffik
3 videocassettes (360 minutes)
PBS Broadcast: Masterpiece Theatre
Crime drama following all aspects of heroin trade from
Pakistan to western Europe.

**The War on Drugs: Heroin, Cocaine, Crime, and
Public Policy**
by James A. Inciardi
Mayfield Publishing, 1986

**The War on Drugs II: The Continuing Epic of
Heroin, Cocaine, Crack, Crime, AIDS, and Public
Policy**
by James A. Inciardi
Mayfield Publishing Company, 1992

Index